TO THE MINER BORN
A STOCKBROKER'S LIFE IN THE BALLARAT GOLD RUSH

Copyright © 2015 J I Kincade. All rights reserved. No part of this book may be reproduced, stored in a retrieval system, or transmitted in any form or by any means, electronic, mechanical, photocopying, recording, or otherwise, without the prior written permission of the Copyright owner.

www.totheminerborn.com.au
ISBN 978-0-646-94557-6
Published November 2015
Revised April 2019

Front cover: Kruger, Fred (1882). Mechanics' Institute and "Corner", Sturt Street, Ballarat. State Library of Victoria Picture Collection

DISCLAIMER

Every effort has been made to ensure that information in this book is accurate, including where possible sourcing information from documents "of the day" such as published obituaries, newspaper articles, wills, and probates. Where possible genealogical information adheres to accepted best practice of determining, at least, two source confirmations. Intrinsic to this book is the use of digitised versions of historic newspapers, however not all newspapers have been digitised and not all search indexes are complete, therefore not all information may be available online or offline. It is always possible that mistakes can occur, things change and improvements can be made, however, no responsibility can be accepted for any loss, injury or inconvenience sustained by any person using this book or by any business, organisation or individual featured in this book.

With thanks to the family gene pool

For my family

Dedicated to the memory of my
Great great grandfather
Thomas C Thomas

Acknowledgements

I would like to acknowledge and thank the following people for their help in making this book come to fruition: my family and friends; thanks to Kal Gould for assistance and local information at Mount Egerton; thanks to Keith Morris at Segontium Searchers for assistance with Welsh records; thanks to the management and staff at Ballarat General Cemeteries and staff at the Ballarat Gold Museum.

Special thanks to Peter Griffiths for editing assistance and historical fact guidance which was invaluable.

Contents

Llangynwyd, Wales	1
Flocks of gold	**4**
The Gentry Landed	7
Eureka!	10
The New Social Divide	13
The Question of Ownership	15
Land to Egerton	**19**
The Legend of Kangaroo Bob	21
Getting In	24
Leaving Llangynwyd	26
The Story of William Thomas	28
Luck versus Skill	33
All the Young Dudes	36
The Ballarat Frontier	**41**
The Morning Light	43
Wild Bill	45
Bust to Boom	48
Barbara and the Prince	55
Life at The Corner	**59**
Limiting Liability	61
New Investors, New Rules, and a New Home	65
Craig's Royal Hotel	72
The Story of Martin Loughlin	75
Mining Disputes and Successes	79
World's Richest Goldfield	81
The Learmonth Gold	**83**
Egerton Gold	85
The Puddling Company	88
Scotland Bound	90
Learmonth vs. Bailey	92
The Quarry, The Rose and The Sister Rose	102
The Story of William "Weeping" Bailey	106

The Story of Owen Edwards	109
A Eureka Story	112
Captain Moonlite and Other Outlaws	116

A pub, The Corner and politics — 119

Egerton Regroups	121
The story of William Mabon Abraham	124
The Story of Edwin Witherden	126
Benevolence	129
Feme Covert	132

The turbulent 1890s — 139

Give Me Land, Lots of Land	141
The Principal Losses	144
The Story of Benjamin Fink	146
The Resilience of the Ballarat Mines	150

The Ajax and the Birthday — 153

Berringa	155
Daylesford	158
The Miners Rest	160
Graveyard Reef	163

The Members of the Ballarat Stock Exchange 1889 — 179

Sources	209
Index	213

LLANGYNWYD, WALES

In the Llynfi Valley of Southern Wales, the tiny village of Llangynwyd lies in the lowlands to the south of Maesteg. At the foot of the ruins of a forgotten castle and roman camp, the village itself is nestled amidst green pastures on a plateau surrounded by gently rolling hills. In its centre sits the ancient sixth-century church of St. Cynwyd's, its grounds home to the largest private cemetery in Europe.

In the early 1800s, there were just a few hundred living inhabitants in Llangynwyd and day to day life revolved around small allotments with enough livestock to feed the tiny community. Life was peaceful, warm in the summer and snow covered in the winter. Although picturesque and historic, the lands of Llangynwyd were not prized for pastoral activities or burial plots. Lying beneath was a real and valued treasure - the lower end of the immense Southern Wales coalfield. At this time, almost all of the residents of Llangynwyd were sustained by mining in some way.

In Llangynwyd, mining was dirty laborious work. Pits were dug by hand with coal carried to the surface in buckets. For the miners working amid toxic gas and noxious dust, extracting coal was tough going:

> As a rule, the pits were large enough to allow only one collier to work therein, and he, having heaved the coal from its bed, brought it up from the pit in a basket, using for the purpose a ladder of sufficient length.
> (History of Llangynwyd Parish, 1887)

Working long hard hours, the miners made a modest living extracting coal for use in the neighbourhood homes. Their job wasn't without risk and, working at around 40 feet below ground with only one way out, they developed a system of working the pits from the bottom up, leaving a hard and sturdy coal mantle at the top providing protection for the workers below. With the inherent risks of the toxic underground environment, the labour of the early miners was not rewarded by the weight of the coal exhumed. Rather it was sold by the sack - threepence apiece – regardless of the size of the sack. It was then transported to the doors in the community by donkey.

As time passed, demand for coal grew throughout the United Kingdom and greater Europe and to meet the demand, mining in the Welsh coalfields exploded. So did the industriousness of the mines. Recognising the value of the coal and the increase of commercial demand for iron, the corporates soon came to Llangynwyd, buying up the land and sinking mine shafts. Donkeys were replaced by wagons and later rail. As a result, the mines got deeper, bigger and more dangerous, requiring more men and longer hours at pitiful pay. The miners turned from small community providores to paid employees of the shareholder companies who took over the coal fields. Accidents were commonplace and often horrific. With corporatisation, the landscape of the area changed markedly. Coal mining became a huge and profitable industry. The community went from self-support to mine support with most of the men employed in mining in one form or another.

In the tiny village of Llangynwyd, one family's name was synonymous with the area, dating back to as early as the sixth century. In the early 1800s, the Thomas family witnessed the transformation of their sleepy medieval hamlet with parishioners numbering just a few hundred into an expansive coal mining community now numbering several thousand. In this Thomas family, there was father William Thomas, a coal pit miner from his youth, mother Amelia Thomas (nee Powell) and their children William Jnr, Mary, Emma, and Tabitha. Their last son was born Thomas Coomb Thomas, his middle name derived from the Welsh translation of "valley" and a name he grew to loathe. Like bookends, he became known as Thomas C. Thomas or just TC to his closest friends.

In 1861, the coal mines and ironworks were operating at full tilt and TC Thomas set off to work. Like most men in his village and like his father before him, he ventured down into the dark fume-filled coal shafts, shovel in one hand and lantern in the other. He was fair haired, fair skinned and blue eyed but in the black noxious dust of the mines unlikely to look anything like that at the end of his 14-hour, six-day a week shift. He was just 12 years-old.

Flocks of gold

THE GENTRY LANDED

In any account of the Ballarat gold rush, some understanding of the European pioneering settlers is a must. This story begins with the very first of those Europeans. Up till the 1830s settlement in the new Victorian Colony was contained to areas around the busy shipping ports of Melbourne and Geelong. The lands to become the future City of Ballarat were untouched, fertile and apart from the few small local indigenous communities the area was unpopulated, still largely in its natural state. No city was planned, pastures not considered. Below a dense forest, its pre-historic landscape and ancient rivers were long since buried by repeated volcanic activity spanning back millions of years.

In 1838, a party of Scottish explorers set about trekking into the unknown interiors of Victoria with little more than a tent, a compass, and dreams. Their search was not for a fortune in gold, the deposits of which had not yet been discovered. Instead, their quarry was more rudimentary; they came in search of new grazing grounds for their ever-expanding flocks of sheep and cattle herds.

The party comprised Henry Anderson, William Yuille and the brothers Thomas and Somerville Learmonth. Some 100 kilometres inland they eventually came to Mount Buninyong, an extinct volcano which rose some 700 metres above sea level. Standing atop of the mount the party surveyed the land ahead. What they saw were rich forested lands stretching to the mountain ranges of the Pyrenees in the north and the Grampians further west. In the near distance, they saw pastures – vast, green and lush – perfect for farming and livestock. With supplies dwindling they returned to Geelong but within a year, they had regrouped. This time, they embarked on a journey north that was to be more permanent. Properly supplied and shepherding flocks, within a year each of the parties had taken up "runs" in the new lands of Ballarat.

Anderson claimed 26,000 acres south along the Yarrowee River calling his homestead Waverley Park. His time here though was short, later selling up and returning to Scotland. The new owner, Jock Winter, renamed the run Bonshaw. Yuille took 10,000 acres to the north in what was to become approximately the modern-day Ballarat suburb of Sebastopol, and his land encompassed Yuille Swamp which is now largely Lake Wendouree. He later sold his estate to his cousin, returned to England briefly before once again sailing back to Melbourne where he successfully bred race horses from stables in Williamstown.

Thomas and Somerville Learmonth were sons of Thomas Learmonth senior, a Scottish aristocrat and wealthy merchant trader who at the time was pioneering the wool trade in Tasmania. Dispatching his four sons John, Thomas junior, Somerville and Andrew to the mainland in search of grazing lands for sheep, his eldest son John settled near Geelong and built a homestead joined later by Andrew. Having made their trek to Mount Buninyong, Thomas junior and Somerville settled on some 45,000 acres and set about raising livestock as new Victorian pastoralists. Their land became known as the Learmonth Run.

Without an official title system yet in place in Australia, none of the new pastoralists made any purchase of the land; they were merely squatters without legal rights or recognition as owners. They simply assumed the boundaries of their runs. As pioneers, the pastoralists were encouraged by the new Colonial government to develop and prosper but in legal terms, their squatted pastures were owned by the English Crown. The indigenous were more or less held in the same position despite having occupied the land for possibly thousands of years prior. Such had been the system of land occupation for millennia, including England, the Americas, Asia and most of Europe. While historically global land often changed hands by war or force, many nations saw land develop through occupation. Australia was by no means to be unique in this respect.

As the Australian squatters had made no financial outlay, neither did the Crown contribute to their development endeavours. However, develop their estates they did, laying crops and putting in livestock. With the advent of the gold rush, recognition of ownership quickly became a burning issue. After some fervent protests recognition did come, about a decade later, as new laws allowed the pastoralists pre-emptive rights to official pastoral leases. As inland Australia expanded, the next 20 years saw the squatters take hold in Victoria. Vast runs were assumed, livestock raised and crops cultivated. Homesteads were built and the runs formed their own identities. Farm labour came in the form of the indigenous, early immigrants and ex-convicts.

As early settlers, the Learmonth brothers were, by 1850, squatters with secured pastoral leases. They improved their run, spread further up into New South Wales and west toward South Australia, amassing huge tracts of land upon which they expanded their sheep flocks and cattle herds. They built a stately residence - the mansion of Ercildoune west of Ballarat and by this time they had the finest Merino sheep flock in the colony. Life seemed rosy.

EUREKA!

1851 was to mark an abrupt change in the squatters' push to pastoralisation. Hot on the heels of gold discoveries in California, it was noticed the lands surrounding Buninyong were remarkably similar to California and not unlike those of the newly discovered goldfields in central New South Wales. Then, while tending the sheep in the paddocks of the squatting Ballarat gents somebody did the inevitable, they dug a hole – and found gold. A few people made claim to being "the first" as government rewards offered an incentive to early goldfield finds. In time, however, the more notable impact of the first discoveries was that they sparked the largest sudden mass migration to a small country area ever seen in Australian history. The gold rush had begun.

In the months following the first discoveries, would-be miners descended on Ballarat in droves. Donning chambray shirts and dungarees and coming from all walks of life were politicians, civil servants, ex-convicts, farmers, and of course emigrants from England, Europe, Asia and the Americas. At one point the exodus from Melbourne was so great the government was using the funds raised from gold revenues to increase civil servant wages such that adequate administration and policing of Melbourne could continue.

For the squatters like the Learmonths, the sudden influx of gold miners turned their once serene paddocks into a beehive of human activity. Without regulation, the miners could pretty much pitch a tent where ever they pleased, and then standing shoulder to shoulder on the banks of rivers and gullies they panned for fine gold and dug for nuggets. Gold was there for the taking and a wholesale free-for-all of frenetic small-scale mining erupted as far as the eye could see. Within two years Ballarat was awash with miners racing from one gold strike to the next. Often small areas reported populations of a few hundred one week and desertion the next as the miners moved quickly from one gold strike to another. Gold fever had taken a firm grasp.

Conditions on the goldfields were by modern measures deplorable. In-fighting was common and mining practices tested the borders of safety. Within the itinerant and fast-growing community, there were no basic services such as sanitation and medicine and while water supplies were plentiful they quickly became choked with sludge produced from gold sluicing. Disease ran rampant and unchecked. Grog tents sprung up everywhere and so did widespread lawlessness. The government responded by recruiting a local civil constabulary to be funded by the introduction of expensive mining licenses. These licences had to be produced on demand as proof of a right to mine. Failure to do so was dealt with swiftly, often with a heavy hand and sometimes with brutality.

The difficult task of providing some sort of legal system and protection to Ballarat's now burgeoning population, the mining licence system was seen by the miners as a tax for the provision of policing. Still the miners had no say in how the area was governed. They quickly grew impatient and rampant abuses of the system followed on both sides. Many refused to pay the licence fees and living in fear of retribution, the area risked descending into straight out anarchy.

The pinch point came in October 1854 when a miner named James Scobie was murdered at Bentley's Hotel in Ballarat. The following inquest and judicial inquiry were viewed by the miners as biased in favour of the accused. This enraged the already tested mining community. Taking justice into their own hands, the miners then rallied against the Crown and amidst riots, the hotel was burned to the ground.

A month later the miners' objections were justified when the alleged murderers were tried and convicted. But the result did little to defray the anger of the vanquished miners. A perception that local law enforcement was biased and futile reigned and relations between the troops and the miners sank to new lows. The miners wanted a say in how their area was to be governed. "No taxation without representation" was the cry echoed throughout the goldfields. All the while the debate over mining licences grew bitter and the heavy-handed actions of the constabulary continued.

The turning point came in the form of the Eureka Rebellion in December of 1854 when, with tensions at boiling point, the miners united. In a rebellious move, they fortified themselves within a crudely built stockade and defiantly burnt their licences. Melbourne sent troop reinforcements and the miners dug in. Then in the early hours of December third came the shocking events – the troops attacked the stockade and the miners responded in battle. Within a half hour, 27 lay dead and many others wounded. Hundreds were arrested to be tried for sedition and treason. Over the coming days in the wake of widespread shock, public support for the miners grew rapidly. If ever Australia could lay claim to having witnessed civil war, the Eureka Rebellion was it. Lasting less than an hour it was to become a pivotal point in the history of the new Colony.

After the rebellion the miners secured not only a fairer and cheaper system of mining rights, they also secured the right to vote. The driving force behind the movement came from Peter Lalor who emerged from the rebellion as both the miners' defender and the champion of Australian Democracy.

THE NEW SOCIAL DIVIDE

As the rebellion heralded in the new era of democracy, the diggings returned to normal life albeit on much fairer and organised standings. With the issue of miner's rights over licences now settled, the debate over land ownership resumed.

The squatters, for all intents not involved with the uprising, continued to expand their stations while still contending with mining activities all over their runs. For them, the new question was more basic. Who exactly owned the land upon which they grazed sheep and the miners dug holes? While many of the squatters had paid for pastoral leases, what rights did they have?

For the Learmonth brothers, their pastoral runs had proven very lucrative in terms of wool production with their stations reportedly generating around £200,000 per annum, a huge amount in the early days of the new Colony. However, the new post-Eureka landscape had set in play a firm divide between the working-class miners and the now wealthy squatters. It was a new social divide the pastoralists, including the Learmonth brothers, felt first hand. In what became known as the "Squattocracy", they were subject to social and political exclusion which they deemed to be most likely based on envy. For the miners, the squatters were likened to the zealous landlords of their homelands, particularly that of Scotland and Ireland.

To rally themselves, the squatters formed their own support networks. A new group called the Melbourne Club rose to prominence and saw many of the squatters as early members. Other like clubs sprang up in regional areas. The squatters now had not only the ears of the like-minded but also the means to exert political pressure.

However, the social division between the miners and the squatters grew daily, especially in later years where mining leases on pastoral lands meant negotiating with the squatters on commercial terms. The squatters, including the Learmonths, usually allowed mining on their runs in exchange for a royalty on any gold found, often between five and ten percent. In monetary terms, what the miners had won in Eureka they risked losing in royalty payments but at least this time it was based on actual gold found rather than just the activity of prospecting.

THE QUESTION OF OWNERSHIP

In the 1860s possibly the most influential piece of Australian colonial legislation was brought forward in the form of the Duffy Land Acts. At this point much of the fertile grazing and agricultural lands of New South Wales and Victoria were locked up by the squatters under pastoral lease. In an effort to encourage inland settlement, the Acts allowed "free selection before survey" whereby those with limited means could purchase small lots of Crown land cheaply for the purpose of farming and settlement. Included in the lands for selection were areas held under pastoral lease – leases that by this stage were nearing expiry.

The Duffy Land Acts were drafted by the Victorian politician Charles Duffy, himself an Irish-born Catholic immigrant who had seen firsthand the repressive and discriminatory system of land ownership in place in much of the United Kingdom. In enacting the Duffy Acts, Australia was prevented from falling into a system of tenant farming whereby small farms were rented from the large acreage estates generally owned by the aristocracy. In England, with no freehold ownership, the tenant farmers were subject to the whims and in many cases, abuses of the land owners. Rents were high as were eviction rates. This system wreaked havoc in both Scotland and Ireland in particular during the first half of the 1800s. In Scotland, the need for increased sheep grazing land led to the horrors of the Highland Clearances and in Ireland the Potato Famine devastated a population whose only means of support (including paying rent) was entirely dependent on the cultivation of their small acre tenancies. Despite Ireland simultaneously producing tons of crops bound for England and Europe, a million Irish died from starvation. In both Ireland and Scotland millions more were left homeless and destitute. In many cases, immigration to Australia was seen as a panacea to their homeland plight and many answered the call.

For the immigrants, the Duffy Land Acts offered the previously unattainable ability for the common man to own land free from rent and feudal rule. As such emigration from Europe found a floodgate. While free selection seemed like a holy grail for the impoverished Europeans, it completely ignored the rights of the existing indigenous communities. The effect of the Duffy Land Acts and subsequent amendments let loose another wholesale free-for-all and would-be settlers embarked on a land rush. Again, the squatters faced the question of land ownership and this time their runs were eroded legally, permanently and often without fair compensation for the developments they had made. Abuses followed. Many of the squatters worked the system using agents or bogus settlers to make land applications in order to secure back their own runs, particularly where there was gold involved. For the second time, they effectively had to pay for their land. The Acts were again modified to counter the abuses and to address the problems faced by the new settlers with many having inadequate means to develop the land under the stringent rules attached to the selection.

For the Learmonth brothers and many other early pastoralists, the Land Acts were possibly the beginnings of the end for their life in the colonies. Having built homesteads, developed pastures, and forged agricultural markets, as well as providing employment and benefits to hundreds of early Victorians including the indigenous, social exclusion and the gradual threat of their prized possession, the land, hit hard. Their vast and prized sheep flocks, and valuable wool clip destined for English and European markets, while generating a profitable income, bore little influence on land ownership.

By the early 1850s, Thomas Learmonth senior had left Tasmania and returned to England where he took over the maternal family pastoral estate of Park Hall in Scotland. Ironically by then the Scottish economy was in a downturn, suffering from the impact of high quality and cheap wool imports from Australia and New Zealand, the very industry the Learmonths had helped to create.

Thomas junior followed suit, leaving Ballarat in 1868 to return to England. Brothers John and Andrew also commuted between their Victorian estates and their ancestral homelands. However, during the next few years, a long shadow prevailed over the Learmonth family in both Australia and England. Thomas Learmonth senior died and under the rules of primogeniture, Thomas junior took the reins at Park Hall. Son John died soon after in 1871 in England. Andrew had also returned to England. For all intents, this left Somerville Learmonth largely to deal with the Australian estates. He too soon felt the call of home and amid a period of depressed economic conditions in Ballarat, doubt over their lands and family death, the Learmonths commenced their exit from the Colony for good, ending a 30-year era of pioneering enterprise in Australia.

To say the least, the Learmonths earned a large fortune from their early adventures in Victoria. With thousands of prime acres under pastoral lease, from Geelong to Mount Gambier and up into New South Wales and generating hundreds of thousands of pounds in revenue annually, they left Australia with a tidy sum. This, of course, came at significant personal and financial cost. However, their contribution to Australian pastoral history cannot be understated, with their legacy remaining in some of Australia's finest stately homes, agricultural and livestock farming areas and significant improvements of once undeveloped land, and their name synonymous with Ballarat heritage. Apart from large pastoral estates the Learmonths also owned interests in the Ballarat gold mines, particularly near Mount Buninyong and some 30 kilometres east of Ballarat at a place called Mount Egerton.

Land to Egerton

THE LEGEND OF KANGAROO BOB

While the goldfields spanned land in every direction around Ballarat, Mount Egerton was somewhat of an outpost, a little too far for most miners who centred themselves in the flourishing mines nearer to town. But a few miners braved the unknown beyond the central mines and by the end of the 1850s, a small community had grown around the mount just beyond the tiny township of Gordon. One of those miners was Kangaroo Bob.

In 1858, few people knew him by his real name, Robert Evans. He was simply known to everyone as "Kangaroo Bob". Irish-born, he came to Victoria in the early days of the rush, around 1856, and pitched his tent in dense woods near Mount Egerton off the then Melbourne Road. A carter by trade and likely fleeing the Irish Famine, in Egerton he followed the dream of many immigrants, his want being to make a fortune in gold and then return home.

Like so many others, initially he had moderate success – enough to get by and feed his family. However, in Egerton he was better known for his dogs that were used by hunting parties in the district to chase kangaroos off the mount. His most notable hound, infamously called "Smoker", was attributed to saving the life of at least one Egerton resident and when the dog was later fatally injured in a contest with a kangaroo, the residents erected a wooden slab above his grave as a mark of honour. It was because of his dogs that Robert Evans became known as just Kangaroo Bob, the go-to man if you had a "roo problem". And the name stuck.

While dogs were his main passion, pursuit of gold remained his occupation. On the morning of 18 April 1858, Kangaroo Bob set off with his mates Isaac Yelland and Jack Lockhart to prospect for gold at a reef rumoured to lie just north of Mount Egerton in an old abandoned claim on the squatter Gordon's pastoral run. What they found was the beginning of one of the richest gold reefs in the area. After pegging out the ground, some 100 feet, the trio agreed to keep quiet about the find in order to register a claim. The next day Bob discovered that both Yelland and Lockhart had taken people to the claim the night before. Furious, Bob set upon Lockhart who later turned up in town bruised and battered from his indiscretion. Bob then threatened Yelland to never again set foot on the claim. Yelland ignored this and staked out 20 feet of his own right next to Bob.

Bob then went to Egerton to find some men to help work his new prospect. Finding Barney Murphy (proprietor of the Mount Egerton Hotel) and Lockhart's brother William they headed back to the prospect. At the claim, Bob declared "I've kicked both my bloody mates out (Yelland and Lockhart) and there's a place for any four men to come in." Immediately Barney Murphy took off his street clothes and ready to work said "I'll be your bloody mate then" – thus making the partnership official.

A few months later both Jack Lockhart and Isaac Yelland sued Kangaroo Bob for their share of the claim, but the judge found in favour of Bob. Instead, Yelland worked his claim for a while but found no gold and sold out.

In the weeks following the bust-up Bob and his "new" mates dug out nine tons of quartz and took it to one of the batteries in Mount Egerton. It yielded 24 ounces of gold. This was staggering at a time when an average yield of about one ounce per ton was considered very good - and astonishingly they had only dug down about 15 feet. At points they found gold simply jutting through the grass.

Although many didn't believe the subsequent newspaper reports about Bob's find, by the next month word was out and shares in Bob's claim were selling for a whopping £300 apiece. By then Bob owned three-quarters of the claim and was offered £1700 for the lot but he refused to sell. Other hopeful miners rushed to the area and pegged out their own claims on land stretching as far as two miles in any direction. Some failed to find anything – others found a lot. But none was more bathed in gold as Kangaroo Bob.

In the first week of July 1858, to prove his claim Kangaroo Bob walked into the office of The Age newspaper with a bag of gold weighing in at 21 pounds (more than 300 ounces), the product of 20 tons of quartz crushed at Egerton. The naysayers were silenced forever.

The following year Bob hit hard luck. He was still producing good gold but when a business deal went sour, he was declared insolvent, much to the sorrow of the local mining community. He was forced to sell his prospect to an investor consortium. Many others tried to sue him along the way and in one court case, the often-fiery Bob hurled verbal abuse at the plaintiff causing him to be arrested immediately. He later admitted he was drunk at the time and was freed with a warning.

After a while, Kangaroo Bob left Egerton for Melbourne where he tried his hand at hotel keeping and horse racing, but these ventures proved his downfall and he lost all of his hard-won Egerton gold fortune. Over the coming years, his claim changed hands a few times until finally in 1868 when the claim lay dormant, a company was formed by the name of the Kangaroo Bob Quartz Company. It carried a strong shareholder list of more than 100 that read like a directory of men in the district. Many of them were miners from Egerton and also a number of the new gold capitalists from Ballarat. Everybody wanted "in" on Kangaroo Bob's gold reef.

At the time of Kangaroo Bob's remarkable gold strike and with a new post office for the area imminent, there was debate over the proposed name of the new town developing just north of Egerton. In honour of Bob, one proposal was to call the town "Evanstown" however the final name chosen marked the area's first settlers. It became known as Gordon.

Robert George Evans a.k.a. "Kangaroo Bob" died at Wahgunyah near Rutherglen in 1892 at age 78, still noted for his love of dogs. He left a wife and nine children, many of whom were born in Egerton. In his wake, Kangaroo Bob set in motion the beginnings of one of Australia's richest gold claims.

GETTING IN

In history terms, we are often led to think of the gold rush as lots of miners panning in creek beds. If they were lucky enough to find gold, a shout of "Eureka!" was all that was required to excite and inspire their fellow miners. As diggers like Kangaroo Bob and his mates tell a story of grit, determination and a load of hard work aside the harsh realities of gold mining in Australia's version of the American Wild West, there was another enterprise taking shape in Ballarat. Post the Eureka Rebellion the miners were left with not only the right to stake their claims, but they also found those claims a highly tradeable commodity.

From the mid-1850s, on the dusty road in front of Ballarat's Unicorn Hotel in Sturt Street grew a new stockade of other sorts. Here on a daily basis, the miners gathered - not to exchange gunfire or shouts of protest. They gathered to exchange their gold claims for cash and to discuss the latest news on diggings. Most importantly they gathered to connect with the capital they needed to develop their claims. It was known simply as "The Corner".

On any given day at The Corner, mining deals were done on a handshake and anyone could participate. On offer was the opportunity to realise the value of a claim by up-selling its potential to any of the willing buyers. Capital could be secured from the various mining agents and equity given to any of the cashed-up investors. Suppliers to the mines spruiked their wares to the mine owners and managers who were all present at various times. By 1860, men at The Corner on most days numbered in their hundreds. It was the place to be if you wanted to get "in" on a Ballarat gold strike without so much as lifting a shovel.

As The Corner rose in prominence, so did the number of men making it their prime place of business. Largely the group was made up of those who had made their fortunes in gold in the early days of the rush. Many had come with nothing and had slogged it out on the river banks over sluice buckets or in the mine shafts under the streets of

Ballarat. Most were from humble backgrounds – farmers, labourers, European miners. All had an intimate knowledge of mining.

The Corner quickly grew into the Victorian centre for mining commerce. At first trading was an informal arrangement where the men just mingled together, and the deals were done. If you wanted to get in to the success of a gold find you simply sought out the agent who had claims for sale and negotiated a price. Visits from the local constabulary were frequent to settle disputes and quell tempers. Trading was often interrupted due to bad weather. The Corner was also the newsroom of the gold rush. Reports of any new strike quickly made its way to those hungry for information. The Press made good use of the flow, making daily reports possible which were then spread across the nation and overseas.

Within a few years, the regular participants assumed the title of share brokers, modelling themselves on their British counterparts and loosely adopting the rules of the London Stock Exchange. The capital demands of the mines were met and following the introduction of the Mining Companies Limited Liability Act the ventures became corporatised, enabling the trading of shares in mining companies.

In what was essentially Australia's first Stock Exchange, the importance of The Corner to the Ballarat mines was imperative. It provided not only the capitalists and speculators with a central place of business but put miners in immediate reach of the cash desperately required to develop the mines and produce the gold. It also provided the diggers with a fairer means of realising and valuing the equity held in their mining rights.

At various times during the 1860s there were upwards of 2400 registered mining companies in Australia with a combined capital of around £24 million. Most of those companies originated in Ballarat on deals struck at The Corner. It was a period of extreme entrepreneurship in a high stakes game. Mine success was never guaranteed, and many ventures rocketed to fame quickly only to fold just as quickly, often in a matter of weeks. This led to high-risk speculation where the gold output became irrelevant as some investors sought to make money purely on the fluctuation of share prices at The Corner.

LEAVING LLANGYNWYD

By the 1850s, the British industrial revolution was well underway and the coal mines in Wales, now predominantly owned by corporates, meant hard labour at pitiful pay. The Welsh miners wanted more. Coming to the Victorian goldfields from the Welsh coalfields, the Welsh miners had one invaluable resource – the knowledge of deep underground diggings. This was a necessity for mining in Ballarat. As the gold leads transitioned from simple surface dirt washing operations to the more complex and dangerous system of deep tunnelling, tracking the ancient rivers laden with buried quartz meant the miners had to haul tons of rock to the surface for processing. It was familiar ground to the Welsh.

With their mining experience now highly valued, for the first-time miners of all nations could participate in the fortunes on their own terms. The willing and able came with one purpose – to strike it rich. Using their knowledge and skill they could dig for gold in precisely the same manner used in coal production, but the payoff was all that they dug was theirs. The mines were small, the land was free, and capital came in the form of many willing investors with cash to spare. As Kangaroo Bob had shown, a simple miner's right and some willing mates were all that was required in this new land of promise.

Miners often came to the diggings leaving families at home. Their initial intention was simply to sail to Australia, find gold and then head back. The British were encouraged with paid government passage, as were the Welsh, Irish, and Scottish. The Colony thought it would secure much-needed labour.

Like the rest of England, by the 1850s the Welsh mines had fully evolved from small party community coal mining to larger industrialised ventures and the miners no longer worked for themselves. With much of the coalfields now under corporate ownership, job losses increased as did scarcity and poverty. Many of the Welsh miners faced low wages or unemployment. Despite their destination being the other side of the world, they answered the call to the new colony in their droves. With the prospect of months and possibly years away from home the skilled miners boarded the ships leaving their families to fend as best they could.

In the small village of Llangynwyd, William Thomas was one such Welsh coal miner. His days in the coal pits made him an ideal candidate for immigration. He also had firsthand experience of the corporatisation of the coal mines. In 1857 he set sail bound for the new Australian goldfields leaving his wife Amelia and children, including his youngest son TC Thomas, tending the home. Arriving in Geelong he headed to the mines in Ballarat where he took work on the Cosmopolitan claim in Eyre Street at Golden Point. Like many of the diggers his life was itinerant and in the following years he moved from one mine to the next.

THE STORY OF
WILLIAM THOMAS

Arriving in Ballarat in 1857, William Thomas followed the gold dream. Initially joining small working parties and moving from strike to strike he had little success. In the early 1860s, a new mine called the New Enterprise opened up at Golden Point in Ballarat. It was privately owned by the Learmonth brothers. Out on his luck, William Thomas took employment at the mine in return for regular hours and a steady income. As a seasoned coal miner, he demonstrated a talent of mine preparation, quickly rising to the position of mine manager.

However, the next few months proved slow going and progress at the mine was disappointing. Unlike today where mines take years to develop, the Victorian goldfields operated on extremely short timeframes with results expected in a matter of months if not weeks. If perseverance was key in Ballarat, patience was not and like many others the Learmonth brothers quickly moved on. After just a few months and with an uninspiring gold yield from the New Enterprise, the Learmonths decided to sell. They quickly turned their attention to other more prospective mine ventures. In particular, they had secured a claim at Mount Egerton.

With the New Enterprise seemingly a bust, William Thomas was seconded to Egerton and in 1867 took up the position of underground manager in the Learmonth's new Mount Egerton Quartz Mine. Joined by his friend and colleague, William Bailey, they surveyed the mount and opened up new drives in the abandoned old claims. They found gold just about everywhere.

Mount Egerton had been worked since the early days of the rush by miners such as Kangaroo Bob, but by 1860 it was thought worked out. However, as the gold started to flow with the backing of Learmonth money the news soon captured the attention of the Ballarat mining community. Before long the area was awash with miners staking claims all around the Learmonth mine. As further finds were made at nearby Gordon, the news spread quickly. With the backing of the wealthy squatters and experienced managers in place, the Egerton mine also progressed quickly. As the New Enterprise sank, Egerton rose as the jewel in the Learmonth crown and they were back in the golden black.

For William Thomas though, work at Egerton did little to satisfy his own want of gold. Once again, he was back working for a private corporatised venture with no share of the profits. He soon continued the search for his own dreams. In 1868, barely a year after operations at Egerton had entered full swing; he left, leaving behind job security and a guaranteed income. Replacing him at Egerton was a young but already seasoned Welsh miner by the name of Morgan Griffiths. That same year Morgan Griffiths married William Thomas's daughter thus becoming his new son-in-law.

Leaving Mount Egerton, William Thomas did not travel far. Becoming a shareholder and manager of a new mining company, the Kangaroo Bob Quartz Company, he set about re-prospecting and re-digging the reefs of Gordon just a few kilometres north of Egerton. Raising £9,000 from the stockbrokers in Ballarat as well as many of the Egerton miners themselves, and without any majority shareholders, Kangaroo Bob's put William Thomas back into the position he and many of the miners wanted – ownership of the mine and a share of the gold profits rather than just a fixed wage and regular work. It was risky but it paid off as within weeks Kangaroo Bob's started to produce gold and its shares traded at The Corner at a premium.

However, again testing the boundaries of patience in the hunt for gold, for some the yield at Kangaroo Bob's was too small and taking too long. It was a familiar tale for Ballarat's mining managers. Produce quickly or be gone.

Amid insinuations that he had been tardy in the mine's progress William Thomas was ousted as manager, his tenure only lasting a few months but long enough to achieve his prime job of opening up the mine. He left for Ballarat and a few months later he was in the post of mining manager at the new Queen Victoria Quartz mine at Canadian Gully. This time developing the new claim was swift and the gold started to flow. But once again William Thomas ran afoul of the mine owners. This time, he was accused of providing inside information to the stockbrokers at The Corner. Although he publicly denied the accusations, despite being closely associated with many of the brokers including Thomas Bailey, brother of his friend William Bailey, William Thomas quit Queen Victoria in disgust. A pattern had developed in his career.

Unperturbed, within a month he became the manager and chairman of the Cambrian Quartz Company back in Mount Egerton, a claim owned by William and Thomas Bailey on land leased from the Learmonths. The Cambrian adjoined the now highly productive and acclaimed Egerton and Black Horse quartz mines. It was not a panacea. After raising development capital, initial results from shaft diggings at Cambrian were disappointing and six months later the company folded leaving William Thomas once again unemployed. By this stage, he had done well with his investments in the mines but lacked the pot of gold he desired. With little to show in the way of gold riches, all that remained of his mining career was a reputation as a man who could test new mines and find the gold. Digging it was another matter.

After the Cambrian failed, the following months saw him move from new mine to new mine taking various positions in mine management, all with equity participation. Some yielded results, others did not. For all intents, his career seemed to stall. By the following year his apparent lack of results could be explained by more moral reasons.

With his years of expertise in underground operations along with firsthand experience in Welsh coal mining, his views on mine safety and costs led him to take the unusual step of advertising his services to the wider mining community. In May 1869, William Thomas wrote an open letter to the Ballarat Star newspaper expressing his opinion that mine shafts should be arched with bluestone instead of timber. His rationale was that arching the shafts with bluestone would negate the need to keep a party of men underground constantly repairing the timber arches and plinths. Apart from the expense of maintenance, the practice of lining shafts with timber imparted greater risks for the miners as they were quickly degraded by water and knocked out of place, resulting in catastrophic accidents and many deaths. As timber sources thinned in the mining areas leaving a scarred and barren landscape, bluestone supply was abundant. However, it too had other uses, particularly in the construction of buildings which was taking place in fervour in all of the gold mining towns. Shafts with a bluestone lining would take longer to develop but William Thomas thought that like the coal mantles used for protection in Welsh coal pits, bluestone would offer the same in the Ballarat goldfields.

His challenge to the mine owners was simple. He offered to prove his theory by undertaking bluestone arching for the same cost as timber, ensuring that his work would "stand without requiring any repairs". It appeared to fall on deaf ears. Consequently, he resumed his life as an itinerant mine manager and over the coming months found employment in somewhat of a freelance nature in many start-up mines including the North German Quartz Company in Maryborough and the Great Gulf Company at Cambrian Hill. In the latter, he witnessed the devastating effects of the fragile nature of the shafts when a flood took the life of one miner and barely missed 40 others. It is unknown if the relatively low number of fatalities was due to bluestone lining.

By the start of 1870 William Thomas was in his late fifties and working again as manager for the Reform Company at Haddon and later at the Midas Tribute Company at Eaglehawk. Tribute mining became common in the later days of the goldfields and involved small working parties, often working in areas that other miners would not. It was often the most dangerous work, however, the rewards if successful could be high. The tributers did not work for wages, the ventures were generally not corporatised. Any gold found was paid in part to the owners of the land, the rest kept by the tributers themselves.

For William Thomas, life had come full circle from his shallow pick and shovel coal mining days in Wales, through the rush of the early days in Ballarat to the tribute mines in Daylesford. In 1872 while working the Lord Derby Tribute mine in Eaglehawk, he fell to his death when a rope he was using to step from one drive to another came loose. Falling 30 feet, his leg and back were broken, and his heart ruptured. Although there was some speculation that children innocently playing near the shaft entrance had loosened the rope, his death was ruled accidental. He became another in the long list of miners whose lives were lost in the perilous goldmines of central Victoria.

LUCK VERSUS SKILL

> As we have over and over again had occasion to remark, few of our quartz mines have failed to pay while the capital was ample and the management good and few have paid or are likely to pay where those conditions are wanting. (The Star, 24 August 1863)

As the Learmonth brothers were busy tending their flocks, the gold rush continued throughout their run. Not oblivious to what was going on around them, they became active participants via both land leases with gold royalties and in the operation of their own private mines to the south-west of Golden Point and further east to Egerton. Like many others, their gold pursuits had varying degrees of success. It was in the early 1860s and with much fanfare, they announced their intention to vastly increase their investment in the mines around Ballarat. It was widely anticipated that with such capital in place, the success of the Learmonth brothers would bring other large investors to the Victorian diggings.

The New Enterprise mine to the south of Golden Point was purchased for £1,000 and included the previously productive and valuable Spread Eagle and Red Streak claims. Here, they invested heavily in new equipment outlaying £1,200 to install fencing and build offices, raise poppet heads and lay the foundations for chimney pots. On the surface the New Enterprise was a hive of activity, however, the riches of the area lay underground in its as yet unworked deep quartz veins. Progress was slow. After a few months, not much stone had been raised and little gold had been found. With high expectations, the mining community was firmly focussed on the Learmonth endeavours but the community's appetite for news ran hot and daily mining reports became the norm to feed the hunger of the investors and speculators. A lack of news was interpreted as a lack of progress.

For the Learmonths, the lack of news from the New Enterprise mine led to public criticism. It was said they had made the fatal error of assuming that "it was safe to erect an expensive reducing plant without actual exploration of the ground taken up". After several months, the mine had yielded next to nothing and by early 1864 crushing at the mine had ceased completely. The claim lay idle.

Adjoining the New Enterprise was the oldest of the Ballarat quartz mining operations, that of the Llanberis Quartz Mining Company. Llanberis had been producing gold for more than six years and in 1863 alone had crushed an estimated 6,500 tons of quartz yielding more than 2,600 ounces of gold. It was also paying handsome dividends. Its 16 shareholders consisted of Welshman, all coal miners, and early arrivals at the diggings. Many hailed from the village of Llanberis in Wales from which the mine took its name. Following incorporation of the company, shares in Llanberis were so tightly held that in its history very few changed hands. The very infrequent offering of stock for sale at The Corner created quite a buzz and was often preceded by local advertising.

Seeking to reduce their exposure at the New Enterprise, the Learmonths put a proposal to the Llanberis Company to amalgamate operations in the hope of reducing the ongoing capital requirements. Surprisingly Llanberis responded by offering the Learmonths the entirety of the Llanberis operations for £16,000. However, by then the Learmonth brothers had decided to focus their quartz mining interests in Mount Egerton and put the New Enterprise up for general sale. In a twist, the Llanberis Company then purchased the whole of the New Enterprise from the Learmonths for just £3,500. The Learmonths had made a profit on their investment but nothing from the gold deposit.

With the New Enterprise ground secured, the Llanberis Company acted quickly by tunnelling through to join the shafts of the operations with the intention of raising enough stone from the two workings to fully utilise the brand spanking new but dormant crushers in place at the New Enterprise. They sold their own outdated equipment and flush with the new deposits available, along with expanded crushing capacity, their fortunes grew quickly. Llanberis recapitalised and in the following year took 16,000 ounces of gold from the New Enterprise. Its shareholders received fortnightly dividends totalling around £12,000.

The success of Llanberis continued for the next 20 years with a significant amount of gold produced from the Red Streak and New Enterprise claims. The fundamental difference between the Learmonth and Llanberis approach was simple. The Llanberis shareholders were working miners dependent on production for a living. This kept costs low and enabled effective use of plant as necessary. On the other hand, the Learmonths were not of a mining background - they sought ownership and management. The Llanberis management continually expanded its ground and took opportunities as they arose, as well as regularly maintaining and updating equipment by reinvesting capital as required to get the gold. The Learmonths were making a large fortune from their livestock grazing interests and the mining ventures were secondary to their ever-growing pastoral portfolio.

In what may have been a bitter pill, the Learmonths appeared to have opted out of the Enterprise too early and as Llanberis showed, perseverance may have produced the gold so desired. However, the experience added to the Learmonths' move from pastoralists and livestock producers into the world of miners and capitalists. An interest in a mine at Elaine was proving gold and there was always the mine at Mount Egerton to keep the golden embers burning.

ALL THE YOUNG DUDES

Sir, I think that the time has arrived now when we (the miners of Ballarat) should be centralised by having an Exchange where we will be able to conduct all our business on the same spot. I propose that we should have a large room for holding public meetings, and likewise for the miners to meet daily for buying and selling shares, likewise to post all notices appertaining to mining affairs, to be open always to the public, and a suite of committee rooms for the different committee men to meet to transact their business, instead of going about public houses, where they are obliged to spend money. I am not a tee-totaller, but I like to transact my business without the aid of Mr. Bacchus. Supposing that 6000 miners should subscribe 10s. each; we should have one of the finest buildings in Ballarat, where all our business would be transacted, and likewise to show that we (the miners of Ballarat) are not behind our merchants in not having our Exchange. To those who think well of the scheme, I'll be happy to give further information on the subject. Yours truly, A Miner. (The Ballarat Star, 7 August 1857)

Several stockbroking firms had built offices next to the Unicorn Hotel, cementing the position for the brokers at The Corner. In the late 1860s, these offices made way for a grand and ornate building to house the London Chartered Bank giving the brokers ready access to the constant stream of gold bearing miners entering the vaults of the Bank. Essentially stock trading was still conducted outside, in front of the Unicorn's veranda. Millions of pounds changed hands. In one year alone one of the early brokers, Thomas Stoddart, was said to have traded over £1,000,000 of stock. Without clear boundaries, the throng of men comprised mining agents, investors and brokers alike. Stock jobbers made an appearance as principal traders, running their own portfolios of shares and making markets in the shares of the many mining consortiums often with wild divergences between the price bought and sold. Speculators made the most of the position by buying, selling and spruiking the stories of mining success, realised or otherwise prospective. This activity was reviled but unabated in a stock market largely without regulation.

By 1857, it was obvious the trading activities at The Corner needed a more formal approach and it was decided to build a more permanent and secure home for the sharebrokers. With capital provided by a consortium of interested parties including John Basson Humffray (founder of the Victorian Reform League), the first Miner's Exchange was built in the backyard of the Unicorn Hotel in Sturt Street with rooms descending some 40 feet below ground. It took merely eight weeks to build and The Corner's activities moved indoors, if not underground, for the first time. However, the location soon proved inadequate and it lost favour as the brokers returned business to the street. In 1861 the first exchange was abandoned to make way for the rapid development of more stately buildings along Sturt Street and the offices became a drapery shop.

As business at The Corner continued to grow daily, the gathering on the street outside the Unicorn Hotel became a public nuisance. On most days, upwards of 300 men congregated at The Corner, blocking traffic and creating chaos. The call to contain the rabble in the interests of women passing the area caused much debate. Over the coming years, a few attempts were made to provide the brokers with suitable digs. Another building owned by Thomas Bath (former owner of Craig's Royal Hotel) was considered and later it was suggested that a tin shed be erected in the middle of Sturt Street opposite the Town Hall to cater to the outdoor persistence of proceedings.

The second attempt at a permanent Exchange was more successful, with the commission of a formal Mining Exchange in Sturt Street. In early 1865 the drapery shop in the earlier exchange was sold and its new owners intended to resurrect it into a new Miner's Exchange, once again attempting to move activities at The Corner inside. Work proceeded with haste and soon after the brokers moved their operations a few feet down the street from The Corner.

> The now just finished Miners' Exchange is one of the most creditable things of the kind in Ballarat. We have certainly had buildings with suites of offices before, but nothing so large and as complete as the Exchange now fully opened by Messrs Grompton, Child, and Broadbent. The Temple Chambers in Melbourne are superior, but the Chamber of Commerce, in Collins Street, is hardly equal, and certainly no better than the Ballarat Exchange. The Exchange now covers the whole of the area belonging to the proprietors and has a suite of seventeen or eighteen spacious offices, including the second story range in the newer portion of the building. By a glass roof there is an abundance of light in the building. The ample arena of the Exchange affords room for the promenading of a large number of the frequents of change. There is a rostrum for auctioneers, and a door on the western side of the central hall opens into the Unicorn Hotel. There should thus be some reason to expect that these many facilities for business and convenient intercourse will in time relieve The Corner of the crowd, which has so long been a nuisance to the public. (The Ballarat Star, 24 October 1865)

With the success of the new building, there were soon calls for another Mining Exchange to be established in Ballarat West next to the Criterion Hotel. Bendigo stepped up plans to formalise its Exchange operations and in Geelong a Mining Exchange opened in the Victoria Hotel. A similar Exchange was being established in Melbourne, but it did little to move the brokers off the footpaths of Collins Street. In an attempt break up the gatherings, the Melbourne authorities routinely took to arresting the brokers for loitering, but even this threat left the Melbourne brokers undeterred. The likelihood of arrest and a hefty fine was regarded as a mere inconvenience in the normal course of business.

In Ballarat, the second attempt at a Mining Exchange in Sturt Street operated effectively for the next year but the brokers' habitual practice of dealing in the street remained. Soon it was obvious the building had not sufficiently addressed the rapid progress of mining. The melee on the footpath outside the Unicorn Hotel continued with the density of brokers and miners on a daily basis providing a little less than elbow room. Despite the glass roof providing some reflection of dealing outdoors, the hall inside the Exchange became so crowded that it was impossible to conduct business in the cramped conditions. Again, there were calls for the situation to be addressed. Again, the ground occupied by the Burke and Wills Explorers monument in the centre strip of Sturt Street was hotly considered. The Corner was budged but not shaken, the crowd moved slightly east on the footpath outside the new Mining Exchange.

The Ballarat Frontier

THE MORNING LIGHT

Back in Wales, the Thomas family remaining in Llangynwyd had made do, income was scant and relied heavily on the youngest son TC Thomas's continuing work in the coal mines. His sister Tabitha, just a teenager, went to nearby Coity to work as a nurse while mother Amelia worked as a washerwoman for the local coal miners.

With regular work and firm footings in Ballarat, father William Thomas sent for his family in Wales to join him in a more prosperous life in the diggings. In 1866 at age 18, TC Thomas left the sleepy village and coal mines of Llangynwyd forever. With Tabitha and mother Amelia, they trekked north through Wales and crossed the Mersey River to Liverpool. Here, along with 300 other aspiring emigrants, they boarded the Morning Light, a clipper ship and trading vessel familiar with the Australian route. The Morning Light was just one of the hundreds of sailing ships taking on passengers and goods bound for the new colony.

For TC the prospect of a new life far away from the grime of the Welsh coalfields was the want of all boyhood dreams, however, the journey proved much slower than anticipated. Hampered by low winds the Morning Light limped its way south taking a massive 70 days just to reach the Cape of Good Hope on the southern tip of South Africa at a time when many ships were making the entire route to Melbourne in just 60 days. Heading east from the Cape beautiful weather ensued but flat seas and again no wind made for slow progress across the vast, featureless Southern Ocean. It would be another four weeks before they saw land, finally reaching the Melbourne Port in early February 1867 having spent more than three and a half months at sea.

In what may have resembled a water-bound traffic jam, in port were hundreds of ships delivering both goods and passengers to the new Colony from all corners of the world. Not surprisingly many ships were simply moored offshore languishing in the tides of Port Philip Bay, their crews long since deserted for the gold fields.

From Melbourne, TC Thomas, Tabitha and Amelia headed to Ballarat, more than 100 kilometres on foot across the high ranges, deep valleys and flat plateaus, the journey taking a few days walking, or a day by train via Geelong. On the way out, hordes of would-be miners eager to secure their own patch of golden dirt mingled with providores, merchants and traders doing business in the fast-growing goldfields. On the way back miners both successful and destitute joined the constant flow of produce and people and more importantly, gold.

When TC Thomas arrived in Ballarat the population had grown to 45,000 including 16,000 in Ballarat East and 7,000 in Sebastopol to the south. A metropolis was taking shape. A council had been formed, water supplies were nearing completion, gas supplies were on and a hospital was in full operation. Social clubs had sprung up everywhere including the Hunt Club, the Harmonic Society, a horticultural society, a cricket club complete with representative teams and various shooting clubs. Several newspapers were providing daily reports including the Star, The Courier, and the Evening Mail. The new railway, coach and telegraph facilities kept the residents in touch with the wider world while the various courts and constabulary kept the township in order. It was written: "A period of sixteen years has accomplished more for Ballarat than as many centuries have done for places in Europe." For the Thomas family, Ballarat was a far cry from their quiet little village in Wales.

When he left Wales, TC's future seemed set. His father held a position of responsibility as a Mine Manager at Egerton. His brother was also gainfully employed as a miner at Ballarat. However, from the departure of the Morning Light to arrival in Ballarat, the Thomas family situation changed markedly. While TC was blissfully but slowly sailing the southern oceans, his father lost his job and his brother had journeyed down a different path.

WILD BILL

In 1866 as William Thomas was rising through the mining ranks, his oldest son William Powell Thomas, known locally as Bill Thomas, headed along a more uncertain track. Some 14 years older than his brother TC Thomas, in his early twenties, Bill Thomas stood five feet six inches in height with blond hair, grey eyes and a full moustache and beard. He was to become the black sheep of the Thomas family.

Following his father's path, Bill Thomas had made his way to Ballarat arriving from Wales a few months after his father. Already with many years of coal mining experience behind him, Bill joined his father at the Learmonth's New Enterprise mine on Golden Point; however the family reunion ended when Bill fell out with the Learmonths and he left Ballarat for diggings near Adelaide in South Australia.

At the time, women in the diggings were outnumbered by men by a factor of four, even more so in the outlying country areas. For this reason, love and hopes of family life were a miner's pipe dream until much later in the colonial evolution. In the 1870s, in his book The Story of Ballarat eminent Ballarat historian William B. Withers describes the phenomenon of women in the goldfields:

The shout, "There's a woman!" emptied many a tent of besoiled and hardy diggers, for the strange sight evoked instant memories of far-away homes; of mothers, wives, and sweethearts, and all the sweet affections and courtesies they represented, and never with such eloquent emphasis as then.

Bill Thomas was like any young digger, not unaffected by the rare comforts a woman presented. In Adelaide, his lustful pursuits became centred on one woman and an affair took place. There was a problem – she was married - her husband left for the mines in Victoria after discovering the affair. There was another problem – Bill Thomas was also married, his wife and family still resident in Wales.

A few months into the affair and essentially left by her husband to fend for herself, the woman broke off the relationship with Bill and left Adelaide to reunite with her husband in Birregurra, south-west of Ballarat. Unperturbed by the fact that both of them were already married, Bill Thomas pursued her, making his own way to Birregurra via Geelong. After spending a night in the Geelong lock up for a misdemeanour, he continued his journey via horse and carriage to Birregurra, bragging to co-travellers about his intentions to steal another man's wife and whisk her away to New Zealand. Buoyed by hormones and fuelled with alcohol, his bravado led to a confrontation with the woman at her new home. Met with rejection, a scuffle ensued. In a shocking result, he stabbed the woman in the neck, leaving her for dead as he fled.

The woman rose the alarm staggering to a neighbour's house. The next day amidst shocking newspaper headlines and with a wildly angry husband in hot pursuit, Bill Thomas became Victoria's most wanted man. Described as wearing a black suit, Parramatta hat, side boots and an Inverness cape, Bill Thomas was tracked on foot through the day and into the night. Mounted police from Winchelsea and Colac searched the areas from Mount Hesse to Cressy to no avail. The husband, on the other hand, went straight to Ballarat and to Bill Thomas' known haunts in the pool halls of the various hotels. Bill's fate would depend on who found him first.

Five days later the husband caught up with Bill Thomas at Mount Egerton where he had taken refuge among friends and family. In what could have been a more perilous outcome, Bill was eventually persuaded to hand himself into the authorities at Buninyong. The woman survived; the husband now prevented from exacting a possible gruesome revenge.

Remanded without bail, Bill Thomas was charged with attempted murder and sent to trial in Colac. Two weeks later, his guilt proven by jury, he was sentenced to seven years of hard labour for malicious stabbing with intent. Now ordered to digging of a different nature he was dealt the sentence common of criminals in the goldfields and spent the next few years working on a road gang.

Shortly after his release in 1872, he married again in Bendigo – it is unknown what happened to his first wife in Wales. In the following years, he settled into a more subdued life, raising a new family in Mount Egerton, taking land in the selections and working as a manager in the Egerton mine. In 1890, he was found dead at the bottom of a well in Egerton. His official cause of death was drowning with the coroner unable to conclude if the death was by accident or misadventure.

BUST TO BOOM

The township of Egerton lies some 30 kilometres east of Ballarat just south of Gordon off the main highway and in the 1860s there were several routes to take. Not yet a railway stop from either Geelong or Melbourne, travel by train involved disembarking in Ballarat then a carriage to Egerton via Gordon or for the more agile, a trek on foot. Alternatively, from Geelong, a carriage to the mining town of Steiglitz then another carriage to Meredith and Gordon, or later rail to Meredith then carriage to Egerton. As the mining interests in Egerton prospered, transport links became somewhat easier when the opening of a railway station at Gordon made commuting from the Mount Egerton goldfields easier and quicker although many residents travelled on horseback or horse and dray or simply walked. The roads in and out of Egerton were notoriously bad, deeply rutted and practically impassable in the wet.

Mount Egerton itself rose some 600 metres above sea level and at its base a lush undulating valley provided a cool climate with occasional snowfalls in winter and breezy winds during the warmer summer months. Standing a hundred metres lower than Mount Buninyong to the west, the terrain from the mount across to Lal Lal and down to Elaine was heavily timbered.

The original settler and from whom the mount got its name was George Egerton, who first explored the area in 1838. Along with others, he followed the East Moorabool River north in search of good sheep runs, finally settling on the banks of Bungal Creek which was nothing more than a semi-reliable spring. From there he set out some 18,000 acres for sheep grazing, calling his station "Bungal" from the aboriginal word for "divided" and it was known locally as the Bungal Run.

In the wake of the first gold discoveries in Ballarat, one of George Egerton's shepherds by the name of Alexander Russell discovered the first of the Egerton gold in a gully called "All Nations" on the eastern side of the mount. A gold rush followed and by the end of the next year, the mount was alive with miners. Kangaroo Bob made his famous strike in 1858 and others had sporadic success. Over the next decade miners came and went like so many other places and Egerton's population ebbed and waned as a result.

In the early days, most mining on the mount was alluvial where the gold deposited in clays was worked out by simple sluicing. From 1854 onwards many parties had taken up claims stretching from Gordon to Egerton, including many spots up and down the mount. One of the early mining parties included David Syme, who after leaving the diggings hung up his shovel and went on to found The Age newspaper in Melbourne. By the end of the decade, it was apparent that the real gold at Egerton lay buried well beneath the surface of the mount in gold-laden quartz veins. It was hard to get and hard work getting it.

By 1860 rock from the early discovered quartz veins was usually sent to Gordon for crushing in one of the area's 27 known small commercial batteries. Depending on the condition of the dirt road to Gordon and whether a cart load of rock could actually traverse it, crushing cost between £3 and £7 a ton including cartage. The gold yield was typically two or three ounces per ton with estimates of the loss of gold to tailings around a quarter ounce per ton. In the dry season when the road was passable, this represented a small profit but in the wet on the heavily rutted road, moving Egerton gold became a loss-making exercise. As such, in comparison to other leads, early production costs from Egerton were very high and many of the miners only generated enough to "buy tucker". Reworking of the tailings of Egerton gold at the Gordon batteries proved highly lucrative for many years, particularly for many Chinese working parties.

Emerging from the initial rush of the 1850s some small operations persevered at Egerton with some parties having installed their own crushers, but the lack of water was a major problem. Water was an essential part of any gold mining activity, however unlike most of the goldfields, Egerton had no naturally abundant water supply, which usually came in the form of a nearby river or creek. At best Egerton's water supply was still the ever unreliable and seasonal Bungal Creek. Over the years, it too became choked with mining silt.

At its alluvial peak of 1857-58 the population of Egerton was around 600, all miners, but over the next 18 months, as alluvial gold finds dried up, most of the miners had moved on to other parts including nearby Gordon. By the end of the decade there were only a handful left, most of them old timers who had finished with mining or the faithful few who remained chipping away at the hard quartz that lay below the clays.

The new decade dawned in 1860 and Mount Egerton arose with new hope. The mining stalwarts had found success in their quartz veins and the area once again drew interest. Over the coming months, the gold frenzy returned, this time with capital from Ballarat investors enabling quartz mining in the deep leads to gather pace. As the quartz veins were tracked to the source deep underground Egerton's real value was revealed.

When the Learmonth brothers purchased the Egerton mine in 1863 they set about establishing the Egerton Quartz Mining Company. Competition for labour in Ballarat was intense between the squatters looking for agricultural workers and the mine owners looking for miners. With more lucrative pay and a chance to participate in the fortunes of the mine, the mines generally won out. In Egerton a willing workforce was available and the Learmonths moved the mining operations from humble and shallow surface diggings to fully mechanised extensive underground shaft mining. The miners swarmed back and by 1864 Egerton numbered several thousand. The township was developing into something more permanent as the tiny community swelled. A post office was built, schools, shops and as many as 11 hotels catered to the needs of the growing population.

The Egerton Quartz Mine developed at a steady pace. The horse-powered whip and whims were replaced by steam-powered engines and several quartz crushing batteries were erected to stamp the rock into smaller and smaller pieces. The stampers ran around the clock six days a week and Egerton residents became so accustomed to the circadian noise that they were often alarmed and awakened at night if the batteries stopped, causing everything to suddenly become eerily quiet.

As in Ballarat, by this time, many of the miners had settled for regular paid work as was afforded in the Learmonth employ. As such they were able to settle down and raise families having the regular income to support everyday life. Work in the mines was harder and riskier but was paid better than farm work, as well as providing the opportunity for more pay if the mine was successful. Many small claim holders gave up their rights in return for regular income and many went on to become equity holders in the thousands of companies and consortiums in the diggings flourishing in Ballarat, Bendigo and beyond.

To the small Welsh ex-coalmining community resident in Egerton, life was pretty similar to the home country, albeit with better prospects. Egerton had comparable weather, similar hills and vales and above all else, by this stage, deep underground mining - something to which they were entirely accustomed. Many still spoke their Welsh native language and socially the close-knit community rallied together. They worked together, played together and sang together alongside their compatriots from England, Scotland, and Ireland. There was also a strong Chinese community. Egertonians came from all walks of life but no matter what the nationality the goal was common, the relentless pursuit of gold.

On arrival in Egerton in 1867, TC Thomas's prospects were less shiny. Presented with the news that his father had left Egerton and his brother was now an incarcerated criminal, it was a far cry from the promise of a settled mining life thought of when he left Wales.

GREENFIELDS OF GYMPIE

Miner numbers in Ballarat had reached saturation by 1867 when news of a gold discovery at Gympie in Queensland sparked new hope and a new rush. By the middle of the following year, thousands had left Ballarat in a trek north to the new digs. Despite work at Egerton being plentiful, among the ranks of the Gympie-bound was TC Thomas who joined the procession, swag in hand, to see if the new fields held as much fortune as the news reports suggested.

Gympie offered the return to alluvial mining and the opportunity of shallow digs and traditional river panning favoured by the old timers and those without the want or need for heavy equipment or salaried regular employment. At the time, the mass departure was seen as welcomed relief for the mines in Ballarat where the number of miners had swollen to the point where labour was beginning to outweigh the jobs available. Unlike the thousands of new immigrants making their way to Melbourne in search of a new life, many of those who came to Ballarat and surrounds came for the sole intent of finding fortune before returning to their homes and families abroad. They had come half way around the world so further travel half way across Australia was not daunting. Gympie was yet another opportunity for the early and seasoned diggers and the late comers too.

The effect of the Gympie rush on the local share market in Ballarat was profound and to some extent caused the first market crash. As the miners left, they cashed in and set their sights on Queensland, dumping their shareholdings in the local companies to any willing buyer at any price no matter how low. With the miners trekking north, the investors followed and expecting a similar boom in Queensland to that of Ballarat, the opportunity to get in on the ground level of a new goldfield was tempting beyond measure.

Within months though, news of the Gympie finds started to filter back – and it wasn't the golden picture many had anticipated.

> In a word, the place is over-rushed and overestimated. There are some extraordinary rich reefs, but still nothing to warrant so large a rush. There are thousands of men walking about doing nothing. The general aspect of the town is anything but encouraging, no money spending, very few amusements, and everything very dull. (Ballarat Star, 19 August 1868)

The Gympie excitement spanned less than a year and the whole event made the Ballarat investors wary. Many had sent their money north to feed the capital monster of new gold mines, expecting a similar scenario to what had played out in Ballarat in the decade past. Gympie was a short-lived boom followed quickly by a large bust. For the vast majority of the Ballarat miners no fortune was found and with the investors many fortunes were lost. Licking their wounds, the investors retreated to the more reliable Ballarat and Bendigo digs. Trading in local stocks resumed with pace and the market recovered from the temporary blip.

With Gympie a bust, the slow trek back to Ballarat seemed the only option for some miners, now out of work and out of luck. Some more adventurous headed further north to Rockhampton and Charters Towers, but many departed Brisbane headed for New Zealand to new finds there.

Like many others who were unsuccessful, TC Thomas made his way back to Egerton to family and friends. By this time the Egerton Mine was in full swing and for TC work was once again very much a family affair. His father William Thomas, his friend William Bailey, and his new brother-in-law Morgan Griffiths largely made up the management of the local mines, his cousin Abraham Abraham the Egerton Mine's blacksmith.

Abraham was a prominent figure in the family and in Egerton acted as key interpreter for the largely Welsh-speaking community.

After an accident left him with a disability, he hung up his blacksmithing tools and went on to write for the Evening News and Ballarat Courier as a correspondent for the Egerton and Gordon area on municipal and political matters.

Now back in the bosom of his family and friends, at just 20 years of age, TC Thomas resumed mining, setting off again each morning to hammer out the veins in the deep shafts of the Egerton Mine. Among the similarly disposed Welsh miners - he fitted right in. With a job secured, next was to find a wife and raise a family in the heart of his newly transplanted Welsh community.

BARBARA AND THE PRINCE

A highlight in the history of the young Ballarat came in December of 1867. The gold riches of the town by this time were known worldwide but possibly the first stamp of credibility came when a visit by His Royal Highness Prince Alfred, second son of the reigning Queen Victoria and second in line to the throne, sparked a sense of town pride. It was the first royal tour of the new Victorian colony. Ten years earlier Ballarat was little more than a sea of tents and shanties housing a rabble of miners and the town would barely have imagined Royal graces, but a testament to the pace at which it had evolved, Ballarat was able to muster most of the grandeur required for such an occasion.

Leading up to the event, everything in the mining town was given the once over. Building activity stepped up in earnest and even the Prince Alfred Hall, which was to be the centrepiece of Royal venues, was completed moments before the Prince's arrival. The creature comforts had not been forgotten with the Prince taking up lavish apartments at Craig's Royal Hotel that had been specially prepared for the visit.

The townsfolk responded with an unaccustomed spit and polish. Men ditched their usual dusty dungarees in favour of full heavy dress suits complete with top hats and highly polished boots. The women sought counsel from the more worldly on the latest European fashions and donned grand frocks that had been imported specially for the occasion, including full bustles, corsets, gloves and lavish hats. The dressmakers and tailors up and down the Ballarat shops were soon overwhelmed.

The days of the tour accompanied weather that was blisteringly hot - not unusual for Ballarat in December but highly inconvenient for the grandly garbed royal watchers. Unperturbed by the heat, for hours the suitably quaffed residents jostled for position on the route to catch a glimpse of the Prince as his party's carriage sped by to the various appointed Royal engagements. Without a breeze to soothe the swelter, the heavily clothed onlookers remained stalwart and proper, if not awkward in their unaccustomed garb.

During the visit, there were grand banquets complete with promenades, dignified speeches and a tour of the working mines of the Band of Hope and Albion Company. A sailing regatta saw most of Ballarat's new glitterati step out as the Prince and his entourage were treated to the best Ballarat could offer. The visit included a sumptuous reception held at the brand-new Prince Alfred Hall, along with a grand Ball to mark the occasion. Of the 500 available, ball tickets could be purchased for a £1 a piece with entry not limited to the socially elite but offered to anyone who could afford the hefty price. The night of the ball was heavy with key speeches and interspersed with song, by all accounts a success despite the stifling heat. Many young women were in attendance - perhaps purposefully paraded for the eligible young Prince Alfred. Turned out in their finest clothes, the bevy of young beauties offered a colourful array of grand evening dresses as well as pretty decoration to the unusually dusted Ballarat society.

Among the beauties at the ball was Barbara Johnson. Barbara had come to Ballarat in 1858 to join her father Anthony Johnson, a lead miner from the tiny mining community of Allendale in Northumberland, England. Arriving in Melbourne along with the steady influx of miners fresh off the ships, the Johnson family headed to the diggings eventually settling in Smythesdale, just west of Ballarat. But the happiness of family reunion was short lived when soon after arrival Barbara's mother Elizabeth died at age 33, succumbing to tuberculosis which was rampant among the mining community. This left Anthony the job of raising his four children, Joseph, Robert, Barbara, and Hannah – all under the age of 10.

Alone among an unruly populace of itinerant miners in a remote area and very little in the way of support, Barbara spent her teenage years making do while her father Anthony worked the mines and did what he could to care for his children. Despite her ramshackle world of male-dominated gold miners in the diggings; Barbara prospered. By age

16 she was making her own way providing nursing support to the sick in her small community at Smythesdale.

However, her life was to take a new route when she became one of a group of young debutantes introduced to Prince Alfred at the Royal Ball on that hot December night. The following day, and in equal heat, a second chance meeting came when several hundred Ballarat children played host to the handsome young Prince as part of the Children's Festival. In a carefully orchestrated welcome and amid cheers of the restless children, Barbara and another 13 of Ballarat's finest young would-be Princesses presented the Prince with flowers. The chance encounters may not have ended in Royal romance for any of the young girls but for Barbara, her introduction to Ballarat's nouveau rich and upwardly mobile signalled that things were on the up.

Then her world shattered. A few months after her dazzling debut at the Prince's Ball, her life took a perilous turn when she was accidently shot by a 13-year-old boy, the son of an ailing woman in her care. The bullet lodged in her cheek and she spent several weeks in the Ballarat hospital while the doctors decided her fate. Eventually supposing it would "work its own way out" the doctors decided not to remove the bullet. Alive, but possibly scarred for life, Barbara returned to her home in Smythesdale to recuperate.

Following her brief encounter with royalty and after her gunshot injury, Barbara found her own prince charming just a few months later when she met TC Thomas, one of the up and comers in society with friends in high Ballarat gold mining circles. Romance blossomed and the following year Barbara and TC were married. Leaving her job and home in Smythesdale, Barbara joined TC in Mount Egerton and from there she set about her life as a new wife in wedded bliss. Or so she thought.

Although Egerton meant a life back in the epicentre of an unruly gold town where women were still vastly outnumbered, the first months of her marriage revealed a less moral past when TC was presented with baby Mary, the illegitimate daughter of a pre-marital affair with a woman who was now a distant memory. Reconciling this news in 1870, among a small and deeply religious community, would have raised consternation for the newly wedded Barbara let alone her new Egerton family. However, TC stood true and Barbara stood beside him. Abiding his indiscretion Mary was adopted, becoming Mary Thomas – first daughter of TC and Barbara Thomas.

Barbara's father Anthony Johnson remained at the gold mines in Smythesdale, her two brothers Joseph and Robert left for mines in Creswick and her sister Hannah returned to Melbourne where she married. In 1886, and alone, father Anthony also died from kidney disease. Death by disease, accident or lack of medical assistance were just some of the many potentially fatal perils faced by the miners. The Johnson family had now experienced both.

Settled in Mount Egerton with TC's extended family, over the next years, TC and Barbara had 11 children of their own: Emma, Margaret, Arthur, Gladys, Inez, Amelia, Joseph, Raynold, and Frederick. Sadly, as was all too common in the day, they lost two children in infancy. However, the union was happy and productive and, with the support of her new community and close-knit family, Barbara prospered.

Ahead of TC in the marriage stakes was his sister Tabitha. Shortly after arrival in Ballarat, the spirited 23-year-old was among the few eligible young women in the predominantly male population of miners. She soon caught the eye of Morgan Griffiths, a Welshman from Aberdare. Morgan was the son of a plasterer but, like his brothers, Morgan had taken work in the Welsh coal mines before Australian gold beckoned. He had been at the Ballarat diggings for just a year and working as a miner for the Learmonth brothers when in 1867, and following the departure of William Thomas, Morgan Griffiths was appointed the underground mine manager at Egerton, with William Bailey overseeing the operations. Romance soon blossomed and in 1868 Morgan Griffiths and Tabitha Thomas were married in Ballarat. In the coming years at Mount Egerton, they had eight children, all born in the heart of a family-filled and growing Welsh community.

Life at The Corner

LIMITING LIABILITY

When mining was limited to just small claims worked by a few men, the potential for debt was relatively low. It was difficult to raise substantial plant and equipment on claims measuring just 24 feet square and the very early miners used fairly unsophisticated tools, making do with basic equipment usually purchased cheaply from owners of abandoned claims. Most of the miners worked their own claims so employment costs were negligible as many took payment in the form of gold rather than wages. Capital investment was typically a boom or bust scenario, representing at best a capital loan or at worst a miner's credit card.

As the mines grew in size and sophistication, the concept of equity capital (ownership by shares) grew in popularity, with The Corner in Ballarat providing the convenient means of access. On offer at The Corner were two types of equity investment opportunities.

The mining investors were those who made a substantial investment in return for direct equity (ownership) in the mine and a share of the profits. They usually took an active interest in the mine and had a say in the day to day running of operations. They took a share of dividends and profits, negotiated in agreement of the terms of their investment. Most had decision-making capacity through board membership or directorates.

And then there were equity shares, where a mine was owned by a corporate entity, usually a company or consortium that issued shares to whoever had the money to invest by way of prospectus. The share investors typically had no say in the day to day affairs of the mine but were able to sell their shares at the prevailing prices at The Corner – supposedly which reflected the value of the mine. The shareholders were invited to attend regular quarterly meetings, but many didn't.

For the mining investors, the stakes were high as they were often locked in with large investments and no secondary market of freely traded shares. The share investors were much smaller and nimbler as they could buy and sell their shares at The Corner whilst still participating in dividends. In both cases, the investments were highly speculative as getting gold was never guaranteed. On both sides the risks were enormous.

In the early days of share speculation, shareholders in the mining companies were liable for any debts incurred in relation to the mines, regardless of whether gold was recovered or not. This led to many busts as over-extended ventures collapsed and miners struck out. The busts suffered by the mining investors were usually spectacular and some of the notable ones tell stories of multiple fortunes both won and lost in Ballarat. The bankruptcy courts were often filled to bursting point with many miners left destitute and knee deep in creditors. Their investors often followed them into insolvency through no direct actions of their own. The ripple effect of a large investor going bust extended to every investment he had in every mine owned. In simple terms, if a mine failed, the miners lost their income - whereas the investors lost the lot, income and assets alike and not limited to the mine in question.

A key piece of legislation for the mining community came in 1864 with the introduction of the Mining Companies Limited Liability Act. As the name suggests, the Act essentially capped the potential liability to creditors to the amount the shareholder had invested:

> Any shareholder in any mining company registered under the provisions of this Act shall only be liable for any debts, liabilities, or obligations incurred on behalf of such company to the amount of the share or shares for which such shareholder has agreed to subscribe, or of which he shall have become the holder by any transfer registered in the books of the company.

Importantly the shareholder's liability included any unpaid calls on capital. It was common practice in the early mining ventures to issue shares at a nominal value but to only "call" on part of that capital to be paid on the premise that future gold yields would negate the requirement for further capital. For example, a company could issue shares with a nominal capital value of say £5 per share but ask the investor to pay only £1 per share up front, the remaining £4 could be called on at the discretion of the company when and if further capital was required. The shareholder's capital outlay was only £1 but his total liability was capped at £5.

The issue of partly paid shares opened up the market to smaller investors, particularly the miners themselves who had confidence in the mine prospects but limited funds to invest. The process allowed for expansion, should a followed gold find grow or extend beyond originally thought, and further capital could be called from the existing shareholders without the need for more shares to be issued.

A provision in the Act catered specifically to the partly paid shares. A company could register as a "No Liability" company whereby the shareholder risk, as the name suggests, was limited only to the amount that had already been paid up. Failure to pay a call on shares resulted in forfeiture of the entire shareholding. No Liability companies were generally those in the early prospecting phase whose potential was unknown, representing greater risk. As such they had greater challenges in attracting capital and suppliers' terms were often incredibly tight with most allowing credit of fewer than 30 days. For this reason, prospecting was undertaken at a furious pace - in order to prove the gold and pay the creditors there was no time to dally.

The consequences of No Liability were twofold. The setup gave investors and miners a convenient means of exit should the mine not prove – they could simply forfeit the shares and walk away. However, the pace at which the prospectors had to work created shoddy work practices that were often fatal. In this respect, the legislators had created a monster. The new legal framework was short-sighted in that it protected the investors and miners from financial ruin but unwittingly exposed them to enormous physical dangers. Mining accidents became a daily occurrence often with devastating results.

The Limited Liability and No Liability provisions had several other key factors.

Firstly, the protection extended only to those companies that were officially registered with the Court of Mines. As such there was an immediate rush in 1864 for existing companies to become registered and almost all new public companies were registered for this purpose.

Secondly, the Act required all companies to maintain a register of shareholders and stated that transfer of ownership included the transfer of the liabilities. This brought about the official issue of share certificates (or scrip) which showed not only proof of ownership and dividend entitlement but also the extent of the liability.

For the mining investors, it gave some protection to their assets not related to the mine although many were still liable through directorship. For the shareholders it gave an important baseline for share investment – a total loss would be limited to the amount shown on their share certificate. Other provisions in the Act related to bookkeeping, official offices, meetings, and penalties.

The Act essentially transferred some of the risks of the gold rush to the potential creditors, particularly those supplying expensive plant and equipment and especially to the capital-intensive deep lead quartz mines. The suppliers now dealt with an incorporated body empowered to enter into contracts rather than just individuals. As such, creditors sought guarantees from directors who in turn mitigated their risk by making sure that decisions made in the mines yielded results at a manageable cost. In short, effective mine management became paramount. This task fell on the shoulders of the mine managers who in Ballarat, overnight, were catapulted to rock-star status. The experience and credibility of a mine manager became a key factor in the investment decision-making process and thereby crucial in attracting capital to the mines.

Left out of the equation were the waged workers and it would take many years, unionisation and strikes for their wages to be recognised as "credit" and for work safety to be improved.

NEW INVESTORS, NEW RULES, AND A NEW HOME

The early 1870s saw capital for mining competing with new demands for civic works in Ballarat including gas and water supplies, roads and the plethora of planned public and private buildings. As cash became scarce, The Corner brokers saw the first of the economic downturns as capital was sucked from their hands into projects of a more important nature. With Ballarat experiencing a moderate economic depression, the mines needed to find new capital sources.

Throughout the 1870s and 1880s, the rich diggings of the Australian goldfields were creating a buzz on the European Exchanges, especially in London where Australian mining stocks had become the flavour of the day. This represented an entirely new source of capital for the mine promoters back home and a few local mining companies made their way onto the London Stock Exchange. The introduction of telegraphic cable made news from the mines accessible in a timely manner.

However, the fervour for Australian gold mining shares came with some degree of risk. In 1887, a prospectus was issued for a Queensland company called "Mount Britten (Queensland) Gold Mine Limited" with a mine called the "Erratic Star" the jewel in its crown. It turned out to be a complete fraud: the miners had dubious mining experience, the existence of gold-bearing ore was not proven, and the land was not even owned by the promoters. Still, the prospectus managed to secure £115,000 from London investors. Such were the heady days of early speculation. Qualitative analysis was passed simply if the mine was in Australia. Quantitative analysis amounted to consideration of how much gold had been found in Australia, perhaps on the assumption the entire continent was just one big gold mine. Therein the overseas investors found a sound reason to plough money in.

Ballarat stock prices were reported each day in the Ballarat, Bendigo, and Melbourne press and loosely derived from reporters turning up at The Corner late afternoon. Information on stocks of interest was swapped between the relevant brokers and reported, the result typically being a line in the news columns the following day showing that a company had buyers at so many shillings/pennies and sellers at so many shillings/pennies. There was no official closing price. This led to wildly different spreads between brokers and a considerable amount of late price propping in the knowledge that quotes would be scrutinised by investors the following day. This was an issue. Facing criticism for the spread variation from the local press and investors, the members of the Ballarat Exchange resolved to bring some uniformity to the process. It was accepted that only trades up until 4pm could be reported and that all such reports were to pass through the chairman of the Exchange. Trading would then continue until 5pm but late trades would not be reported. In addition, any broker found giving trading information to the press would be fined £5. This was the first test of self-regulation. Not all of the members agreed and two of its most notable ones, Edwin Millard and Thomas Stoddart, resigned from the Exchange in protest.

In the following weeks, the debate over the new reporting arrangements raged. The brokers were split, and talks rose of a new rival exchange. A week later the debate had become so distracting that a satirical prospectus was circulated among the members proposing the following:

> THE "GO-AS-YOU-PLEASE MINING EXCHANGE"
>
> The president is Thomas Williams; vice-president, William Thomas; directors, Thomas Williams and William Thomas; secretary, William Thomas; list of members, Thomas Williams and William Thomas. The following are a few of the benefits guaranteed to intending investors: All sales will be quoted at any price which suits members of this exchange, and all sales made by persons not members of this exchange will be

> treated as sham ones, and considered utterly unreliable. The press reports will be made a special feature by the present exchange, and every effort will be made to keep up or run down the prices of stocks in which any client (or especially any member) may be interested. It is, however, pointed out that all sales made will be submitted to the president, approved of by the vice-president, and finally passed as correct by the secretary. This will naturally ensure that nothing but bona fide sales will appear in the daily reports, etc. (Bendigo Advertiser, 10 May 1881)

Suitably miffed by the factions now present within the Ballarat Exchange, members Millard and Stoddart responded in the only way they knew how – they opened their own Exchange. In July 1881, to much applause, the new Royal Stock Exchange opened its doors in the rooms of the newly rebuilt Unicorn Hotel. Here they held daily meetings to which the members of the press were welcomed and by mid-July the new Exchange boasted some 150 members. Trading was brisk and the local press resumed their reporting.

There were now officially two Exchanges in operation in Ballarat – the Ballarat Stock Exchange and the rebellious young Royal Stock Exchange operating within metres of each other. Both were competing for the same capital and investors. Typically shares in the mining companies were traded on both exchanges and by the end of September price differences between the two Exchanges were vast, at times reportedly as much as £10 on some stocks. The investor community at large became increasingly irritated. Something had to give.

For a while, both exchanges operated independently but, like many of the mining ventures, the Royal Stock Exchange was catapulted on promise and after failing to deliver it soon became dust. Although now the bigger of the two Exchanges, the Royal Stock Exchange was the first to falter. On a lonely day in September of 1881, after only three months of operation, the Royal Exchange posted its end of day trading results to show that on its list of a hundred or so companies there was but one single trade, in a stock that no-one had ever heard of. The jobbers were deflated, the press bereft. One member at The Corner called that day at the new Exchange a "maiden over".

The barring of brokers talking to the press forced aspiring miners and speculators to become more enterprising. In the early years of the 1880s, there were many scandalous ventures making their way into the news columns by other means. The "salting" scandal of 1880 came about when a couple of adventurous miners turned up at The Corner with two buckets of gold-laden dirt apparently extracted from the Hurdsfield Mine to the south of Ballarat. It was later found that the dirt had been "salted" - a devious activity where gold was loaded into a gun and fired at close range into a mine face. Other scams emerged over the years including the delivery of telegrams containing favourable but fabricated prospecting news to the offices of the local press, sending the markets into a frenzy.

Fearing a backlash from the overseas capitalists and a no-confidence vote from local investors resulting from the ever increasing incidence of foul-play, the Ballarat brokers responded with a proposal that a Board of Advice be formed with active support sought from both the Bendigo and Melbourne Exchanges, and that such advice be attached to each prospectus to attest that the Board considered the contents to be bonafide. Further, in order to increase confidence in the local investment offerings, that notices be placed in the London papers stating that an Investor Protection Society was in existence and available for consultation. This proposal was rejected as unworkable. Despite the lack of an auditing process and the absence of expert opinion, most prospectuses passed scrutiny. Today many of the concepts raised in this proposal have been subsequently developed and implemented in various forms.

In the summer of 1885, the Royal and the Ballarat Stock Exchange merged to form one stronger and more organised Exchange. Along with this, it was decided that a new home would be appropriate, supported by the local community who were still resolved to move the unruly rabble of the brokers at The Corner off the street for good.

A suitable site was found situated on the "logs" in Lydiard Street, the place where unlicensed diggers were chained in the days before the Eureka Rebellion. It was also the site of the government camp from which the orders to attack the Eureka Stockade were issued. In June 1887, on Queen Victoria's Jubilee Day, the townsfolk gathered at the site in Lydiard Street. On this day, three important foundation stones were laid. Firstly Sir John William Clarke, a squatter and pastoralist, laid the stone for the building of the new Ballarat Art Gallery. Next Thomas Stoddart laid the stone for the new Mining Exchange and then Mr. John Murray laid the stone for the building of the Old Colonists Association. With ceremonies done, construction of the three new buildings got underway. All three were to become icons of Ballarat architecture.

In 1888, the new Mining Exchange opened as a grand modern building fit for purpose. Costing £5000 and funded by a consortium of brokers led by Thomas Stoddart and John Embling, the front of the building housed four offices occupied by brokers George Purves, John Reid, Thomas Stoddart, David Binnie and James Horn. Beyond these, there was a large open area for negotiations and 40 members' offices that were available for rent. The architect was C. D. Figgis although the design of the floor space can be attributed to the vision of Thomas Stoddart who found inspiration in his travels to the European and American bourses.

Initially, brokers paid an entrance fee of £50 each to secure membership of the new exchange and by the time it opened, 108 members had signed up thus recouping the original development capital of £5000. At the same time, the original investors recapitalised their venture and raised a further £50,000 by the issue of a prospectus for shares in The Ballarat Stock Exchange, Finance, and General Agency Company Limited. The lease on the land was renegotiated with the City Council and with rent set at £1000 per annum it was duly rolled into the new entity. Annual rents from the building yielded around a healthy 15 per cent making it one of the most profitable privately owned buildings in Ballarat. The committee for the new venture included the initial investors William Bailey, Frederick Downes, David Fitzpatrick, Alexander Gilpin, William Gale, Edward Morey, Felix McGovern,

William Watts, John McDonald, Henry Rawlings, George Purves and Thomas Stoddart.

As well as a new home for the members, a constitution was implemented with new rules bringing trading at the Exchange into line with its Melbourne counterpart. The official list of companies and quotations were removed from public distribution in an effort to curtail the activities of non-members who were using the lists to further their own unofficial businesses. This cemented the one-to-one relationship the members had with their clients who could access information such as news and prices only when in contact with their broker, or by reading the official press. Trading sessions were limited to a morning and afternoon session for a period of two hours each. For the first time companies wishing to have their shares traded on the Exchange were required to pay a listing fee. With the new Exchange opened, finally the days of The Corner were over, and the men disappeared off the street forever.

Over the 33 years from 1855 to 1888, The Corner held a commanding position as the headquarters of Australian mining capital. In that period, more than 7500 mining companies were registered in the State of Victoria at an average rate of 20 per month. Nearly one-half of those companies came into being in the 1870s alone. Not all of them were successful in mining and not all were traded on any of the Victorian Stock Exchanges, however, the large majority were formed from mines in the central Victorian goldfields around Ballarat and Bendigo. The men at The Corner were responsible for most of them. Shares in the 7500 companies were spread across 288,000 individual shareholdings at a time when Victoria's population was less than one million. Less than three percent of those shareholdings were held in the name of women.

Today the third Mining Exchange in Lydiard Street takes pride of place in Ballarat heritage, carefully preserved and maintained. Its fate was nearly thwarted in the 1920s after share trading ceased following World War One and the lease on the land expired. Reverting to the City Council it spent its days as a motor car showroom. The earlier exchanges are long since forgotten landmarks although some parts may remain in the form of rooms under the Unicorn Hotel. In the 1930s the Mechanics Institute annexed part of the second exchange for its reading rooms. The once grand London Chartered Bank on the corner of Sturt and Lydiard Streets next to the Unicorn Hotel suffered a less fortunate fate. In the later 1960s it was demolished to make way for a less salubrious and "modern" Commonwealth Bank – perhaps a most shameful blot on the current Ballarat streetscape. The Unicorn Hotel has recently been revived after a period left in decay.

Of The Corner, nothing remains except in photographs* of the days when the brokers and miners in all their glory gathered on the street to conduct the business of the Ballarat gold rush.

*Author's note: the cover of this book shows a rare photograph taken of The Corner in 1882 by photographer Fred Kruger. From the State Library of Victoria Picture Collection.

CRAIG'S ROYAL HOTEL

When not doing deals on The Corner, and when the weather broke proceedings, the favoured hangout of the brokers was Craig's Royal Hotel, conveniently just a short walk across the road.

Built in 1853 by one of Ballarat's earliest settlers Thomas Bath, its original building was of timber on a block of land purchased for £400 and replacing an earlier construction. When finished the hotel was the largest building in Ballarat and it dominated the streetscape. During the Eureka Rebellion, it became the gathering place for many interested onlookers and refuge for others, providing a good view to the Stockade as it unfolded. In the days following the massacre the then named Bath's Hotel was the meeting place for the various groups sent to assess the situation and a number of officials took up temporary residence. Much of the early testimony and firsthand accounts were taken at the hotel as it became the office of the Gold Fields Commission of Enquiry in Ballarat. In later days the meetings of Peter Lalor's Reform League were held at Bath's as were many other important local organisations, safe to say that a lot of Ballarat's future was decided at the hotel. For many years, Bath's was a central point in the township not only for business but also being the prime coach stop from Melbourne and Geelong with stables added later to suit, as well as the lodging of many notable dignitaries.

In 1857, Thomas Bath sold the hotel to Walter Craig although Craig was not the initial intended buyer. He had been appointed by John Disher, landlord of the Tattersall's Hotel in Melbourne, to value the property. Disher wanted to buy it but later withdrew and subsequently, Walter Craig took the opportunity to purchase the hotel for himself. Business continued as usual under its new name Craig's Royal Hotel, the Royal added in the advent of the Royal visit by Prince Alfred in 1867.

During the 1860s the hotel became the central venue for many shareholder meetings and society gatherings, and it is probable that more than a few corporate deals were struck, many glasses raised, or sorrows drowned, across the bar. It was the first hotel to be granted both a billiard and late licence. It was the adopted home of the Ballarat Turf Club of which Walter Craig was a member. Craig owned several racehorses, indulging his passion for the sport.

Substantially rebuilt and expanded in 1862 to include upper stories and ornate facades, as well as a tower, a cellar and a commercial room, the hotel now took an imposing 65 feet of frontage onto Lydiard Street. The rebuild took several months and employed nearly 90 men. The tower itself became an iconic part of the landscape providing a view across the growing township and the opportunity for local surveyors to officially map out the Ballarat district.

Not only the place to be seen, Craig's had become the influential hub of business in Ballarat with all the movers and shakers of the day in part-time residence including the brokers, politicians and dignitaries both domestic and foreign, as well as hosting royal visits.

Without exception, the hotel was the informal second home to the stockbrokers at The Corner. With its location so convenient, in practice a new mining enterprise could be capitalised over breakfast at Craig's and its shares on sale at The Corner before lunch. The process was informal; often deals were done on a simple handshake with the relevant paperwork dealt with later.

In 1869, Walter Craig's formal relationship with the brokers was sealed when his daughter Sarah married one of the prominent members at The Corner, Thomas Bailey – an Englishman and brother to William Bailey of the Mount Egerton mine. Thomas and Sarah later went on to own the original Prince of Wales Hotel in St Kilda, Melbourne, long since gone and replaced with a more "modern" 1920s version. The Melbourne foray was brief though and the couple returned to Ballarat after the death of Walter Craig. Thomas Bailey who had now amassed his own fortune returned to stockbroking at The Corner.

The heyday of Craig's Royal under Walter Craig's helm ended abruptly when he died in 1870 at age 45. Legend has it that he foresaw his own death in a dream recounted to friends soon after. In his dream, he saw a jockey riding his own renowned horse "Nimblefoot" to victory in the upcoming Melbourne Cup – the jockey wearing a black armband in honour of the recently deceased owner. Fulfilling the prophecy, Walter Craig did actually die a few months before the race and indeed Nimblefoot did win the Cup – the jockey indeed wearing a black armband in remembrance of the recently deceased Walter Craig.

Following his death and as per his testamentary wishes, Walter's hotel was put up for sale by auction with the original owner Thomas Bath acting as trustee for the estate. With a reserve set at £11,000 it was passed in at just over £4,000, a disappointing result and for a while, the future of the hotel was in doubt. Later, its most endeared patrons, the stockbrokers, tried to mount a consortium to buy the hotel as a corporatised share venture but could not raise enough capital in the prevailing economic depression. In the following years, it saw several different owners who made various alterations including demolition of the tower. The brokers continued to frequent Craig's Royal but with less zeal and shareholder meetings that were still held regularly in its commercial rooms generally moved on to other venues.

The hotel still in operation today stands as an imposing landmark and icon to Ballarat's gold mining heritage. With much of its grandeur and elegance intact, it affords a rare step back into Ballarat life in the 1860s. It is said that the ghost of Walter Craig still inhabits its corridors.

THE STORY OF MARTIN LOUGHLIN

Perhaps the rich story of Craig's Royal Hotel can best be elaborated through the account of the life of one of its most notable long-term residents.

Standing an imposing six foot three inches tall, Martin Loughlin was once described as the most handsome man in Ballarat. He was indisputably one of the wealthiest.

An Irish-born Catholic, and an apprenticed baker, his first overseas adventure was as a young lad when he sailed to America in 1852, but the adventure curtailed when his ship was wrecked off the Newfoundland Coast. All were saved but the event saw Loughlin returned to Ireland.

In 1854, he set off again this time to Ballarat to dig for gold. After a short stint working in a shop in Geelong, he arrived in Ballarat in early 1855 and joined the Ballarat diggings. After a while and with some success he took equity in a few of the mines. Eventually, he became a large investor in the highly successful Band of Hope Company, the largest mine in Ballarat which had won more than 230,000 ounces of gold and was paying out large dividends. In its life, the Band of Hope reputedly took over 600,000 troy ounces of gold.

With money behind him, Loughlin then bankrolled many of the region's deeper digs and was soon widely considered the go-to man for mine capital. In the 1860s and describing his occupation as a stockbroker at The Corner, he quit hands on mining and focussed on investing. To this he was very successful and built a large fortune, so successful in fact there was a saying amongst the diggers that "Everything Martin Loughlin touches turns to gold" and often his name alone on a share registry was enough to send stock prices skyrocketing.

Loughlin was well known and well respected in Ballarat, however, his name was thrust into the wider public limelight in the 1870s when he became embroiled in the famous Great Egerton Mine lawsuit. Of the named defendants in the Learmonth vs. Bailey case, Martin Loughlin was already the most independently wealthy by the time case was fought but after the dust settled on its legal issues, the Egerton mine yielded Loughlin another handsome profit despite the massive legal costs: "Each member of the syndicate cleared about £80,000 on his investment. A large portion of the profits, however, were subsequently eaten up in defending a case brought by Mr. Learmonth against the company."

In 1879, in partnership with William Bailey, he purchased the Seven Hills Estate and again the golden riches prevailed at its mines such as Madame Berry, Lone Hand, Loughlin, West Ristori and Lord Harry. He also had interests in the Glengower Estate at Clunes and held pastoral leases in Queensland as well as extensive hotel interests.

Naturally shy, Martin Loughlin may not be remembered as being a great leader, architect or engineer; however, his financial generosity in Ballarat was legendary. Of his civic donations, many remain as valued parts of local heritage and prized cultural significance. Many may well not exist if not for his generosity. To name a few, he made large donations to support the erection of both the Tom Moore and Robert Burns statues in Sturt Street, as well as the building of St Patrick's Cathedral. He partially financed the building of Nazareth House at Lake Wendouree, enabling the Sisters of Nazareth to care for the aged, poor and infirmed. It is still in operation today. His annual donations included many local charities at Christmas and in times of need. He was equally generous towards mining widows and families who benefitted from private bequests.

A trip to his homeland via a tour of Europe and China in the late 1880s revealed his true love of Ballarat and his intended travel was celebrated in both Ballarat and Melbourne with farewell dinners held in his honour. During one dinner at Craig's Royal Hotel he responded to the good luck wishes expressing his sentiments on Ballarat:

> Mr. Loughlin said that he had always endeavoured to do his best for the city and district to which he owed so much, and that when he returned he hoped to be so invigorated as to still further assist in the development of one of the most beautiful cities of the south. (The Australasian, 6 April 1889)

In his travels through Rome, he purchased several artworks to be donated to the Ballarat Art Gallery including Departing Day by Peter Graham, The Sway Inn by B.W. Leader, and Days Loch on the Thames by George Vicat Cole. The bequests then valued at £5,000 or roughly the same amount it cost to build the Art Gallery.

A keen sportsman, his pursuits included hunting with the hounds as a member of the Ballarat Hunt Club. His turf interests saw him as a prominent high stakes figure in racing circles across the country. His interests bore a Grand National winner, a Geelong Cup winner, a Caulfield Cup winner and most notably a winner of the Melbourne Cup with his horse "Sheet Anchor", then a 20 to 1 long shot. This race alone earned Loughlin £24,000.

Despite being well known and greatly respected, he was averse to publicity and shied from public office although he once polled in the Legislative Council for Nelson Province, albeit unsuccessfully. As with most of the stockbrokers and investors in Ballarat, Loughlin lost heavily in the financial crisis of the 1890s with his personal loss estimated to be upwards of £100,000 – almost a third of his wealth.

Martin Loughlin died in the Spring of 1894 at age 61, having been a permanent in-house resident at Craig's Royal Hotel for some 20 plus years. His funeral was the largest the district had ever seen with an estimated 12,000 people lining the route to the Ballarat New Cemetery.

Considered one of Australia's first mining magnates and despite the financial crisis of the 1890s, Martin Loughlin left a substantial legacy. Having never married, his estate estimated to be worth £250,000 was bequeathed to his brother and nephews and many charities including Roman Catholic schools, the Ballarat Hospital, Orphan Asylum, and Benevolent Asylum, and hospitals at Melbourne, Clunes, and Creswick as well as generous bequests made to the Ballarat Art Gallery. Most of his final wealth was in the Glengower Estate and loans owed by his colleagues and friends Andrew Chirnside and William Winter-Irving, both Scottish pastoralists.

Whilst Loughlin's contribution to Ballarat was immense, his only named memorial resides in Ireland. Using funds inherited from Loughlin's estate and honouring his last wishes, his brother and two nephews paid £30,000 to construct a Catholic Church in his honour. Finished in 1903, today the impressive Church of Saint John in Kilkenny is described as one of the most beautiful churches in Ireland and Martin Loughlin's legacy forms a proud part of the Church's heritage.

Of his Irish nephews, Thomas Loughlin's commitment to his uncle's legacy found him favour with the Catholic Pope. Several years after Martin Loughlin's death, Thomas Loughlin and his wife Kathleen emigrated from Ireland to take up land at Warrenheip near Ballarat as "Count and Countess O'Loughlin", a title bestowed by Papal decree. Together they built an impressive mansion called "Killarney" as well as an equally impressive home in the affluent suburb of Kew in Melbourne. Thomas Loughlin continued Martin Loughlin's legacy of charity throughout his life and was a well-known and large benefactor of many of Ballarat's charitable institutions and Victorian Catholic churches.

Not a man to rest on his laurels or idle his hours indifferent to his surroundings, Martin Loughlin's impact on the development of Ballarat left an indelible print that can be seen in and around the city today. Known to the locals as "Big Martin", throughout his life, his personal motto was simple… "When you want a thing well done, you do it yourself."

MINING DISPUTES AND SUCCESSES

Mining disputes were commonplace all over the Ballarat goldfields and special courts were set up to deal with mining issues, namely the Court of Mines. Issues included claim "jumping" which availed any prospector the ability to claim land held under mining rights that had apparently been abandoned by the claim owner. Other matters included boundary limits, issues of underground syphoning and equipment licencing.

Within the claim system, the ground was typically staked out in small areas, some measuring just a few feet square. Claims were easily definable on the surface as the common practice of pegging kept the boundaries clearly marked, but as the mines went underground and expanded in acreage determining exact boundaries was difficult if not impossible. This created real issues in terms of valuation. Those that didn't have the capital to dig deeper lost out and received only the surface value of their claims although some were content with the value assigned to their claim's location rather than actual production. Due to the intensive capital required it was common for such claim owners to delay deep digging until such time as an adjacent and more affluent mine had dug deep close to their boundary and proven the existence of gold-bearing ore. This, in turn, enabled them to raise capital or, as was often the case, sell their claim for speculative profit. It was a risky game. If you did not show the development of your claim it could be jumped. As such there was plenty of activity just moving dirt piles from one side of the claim surface to the other. If you spent money developing the claim it could amount to nothing if your neighbours found nothing, thus rendering your entire claim worthless.

This scenario played throughout the Ballarat goldfields, especially among the smaller claims. It brought rise to what became "address stocks" – those valued purely on what may possibly, or hopefully, be in the ground based on proximity to other known and successful deposits. The scenario prevails today.

The years of mining had shown that what lay on the surface in Ballarat was only a small drop in the rivers of gold that lay underneath in rich gold-laden quartz veins of the ancient river beds and volcanic basalts. The process in quartz mining was fundamentally easy – find a vein and then continue to track it. This always involved digging to depths, sometimes thousands of metres to track the reefs. Water was a problem and many deep mines hit the water table thus stopping progress until the arrival of pumping technology. Often the reefs displayed their very fickle nature by starting abruptly and ending the same and digging just a few feet in either direction could lead to success or failure. It is easy to imagine a miner's determination could be won on the precipice of "if I just dig a few more feet" or lost on the dejection of "did I miss it?" Regardless, quartz mining required a lot of capital and the more capital you had to dig deeper the greater your chance of extracting more ore from the vein.

The potluck nature of the mines is shown in the early workings of the gold fields. At the Red Hill Lead, 1,500 ounces was produced from a claim measuring just twelve feet square. In four weeks of mid-1867, the Band of Hope Company produced 14,900 ounces from one shaft in its claim and comparatively nothing in the weeks following from the same ground.

Over the decades following the initial rush, many of the early mines were reopened over and over as new technologies provided better ways to handle water, transport the ore and crush the quartz. In many cases, the trick was keeping control of the claim.

WORLD'S RICHEST GOLDFIELD

Examples of the explosion of mining and the intense effect of capital are demonstrated in summary of the following four Ballarat companies in the early days:

The Koh-i-Noor Company on Golden Point ran over 170 acres. To the end of 1869, it had expended £286,000 extracting 148,000 ounces of gold valued at around £600,000. It had paid out more than £300,000 in dividends to shareholders.

The Band of Hope and Albion Consols Company working the Frenchman's Lead in Sebastopol and Golden Point lead covered around 400 acres. It had subscribed capital of £450,000 and employed more than 900 miners making it the largest mining company in Victoria. Gold won delivered £910,000 from around 230,000 ounces – it had paid out £648,000 in dividends.

The Prince of Wales Company on Cobbler's Lead at Sebastopol raised an average 1500 trucks of gold bearing quartz per day, employing nearly 400 miners. The company won 128,000 ounces of gold valued at £522,000 paying dividends of £234,000.

The St. George and Band of Hope United Company had a number of claims scattered throughout the Ballarat goldfields covering a combined 250 acres. With subscribed capital of £120,000 and an itinerant workforce of anywhere from 75 to nearly 400 in any given week the company yielded gold to the value of £296,000 and paid out £74,000 in dividends.

In 1868, the value of plant and equipment employed by the Ballarat mines was reported at £706,000, nearly twice that of Bendigo. The Court of Mines held 908 registered Ballarat companies with a nominal capital of just over £10 million.

While exact figures are unknown, the accepted amount of gold exported from Victoria over the 20 years from the first find amounted to 36 million ounces representing a total value in excess of £150,000,000 (with gold at £4 per troy ounce). Production peaked in 1856 at 2.9 million ounces then averaged around 1.7 million per year to 1867, falling to just over one million by 1869. The only other district to rival Ballarat was Bendigo which over the same period produced similar amounts of gold.

The end of the 1860s closed a decade of both frenetic and haphazard activity in the mines and the township of Ballarat itself. Millions of pounds had been won from the gold diggings resulting in prosperity and wealth beyond the wildest of dreams, but the start of the 1870s ushered in a new era of attention focused on civic projects for the now burgeoned populace of Ballarat. Plans for major capital works such as gas and water supplies, roads and public buildings took centre stage. Committees were formed for everything. There were working parties, consultation papers, and non-stop meetings. This led to the inevitable layering of bureaucracy, a paradigm previously unseen in Ballarat. The township was split in two – Ballarat West and Ballarat East. Political tension emerged as bickering between the two Ballarat municipalities saw them fight for power, prestige and capital. The development of the new town hall, the public jewel, led to severe cost overruns and at one point nearly bankrupted the city.

At the same time, the mines were entering the secondary phase; simple prospecting was over, and attention now focused on production and cost control. The mines had matured into fully fledged business enterprises - labour and equipment consolidated. This led to reduced revenues for the local government and business, both of whom had been riding the wave of mine development. As the ambitious public works now competed for valuable capital, money for mining became scarce, stock prices fell, and Ballarat entered a moderate economic depression.

The Learmonth Gold

EGERTON GOLD

The Egerton gold reef was fickle in nature. Many times, it had been worked through, sometimes with great success but often providing the miners with little more than living expenses. From 1854 to 1860 the township itself had already experienced several booms and busts, the population reflecting the short-lived bursts of activity. In 1861 with the field again thought bust it was estimated the entire mount could have been purchased for just £60. By 1863, part of the hill had actually "fallen in".

In 1863, the Learmonth brothers decided to properly develop the field and they paid £7,000 for the whole of the Mount. In buying the run outright and not using capital funded by The Corner it was one of the few privately owned goldmines in the district. The claim covered 24 acres under miner's rights and the Learmonths had secured a 15-year licence. After investing in some plant and machinery they commenced digging the Quarry and Rose shafts. They quickly started to pay. The then mine manager Pritchard reported that yields had been "occasionally satisfactory" and indicated this result was only due to the "constant and steady perseverance" of the Learmonth brothers. Information coming from the mine was limited but rumours abounded.

In 1867, Pritchard again reported on the Learmonth operations stating, "the mine has yielded splendidly for the past twelve months, often 1 ounce to the ton and with every indication of permanency; and at the present time Messrs. Learmonth hold one of the most valuable mines in the colony." It had taken many years but the Learmonths were finally reaping the riches of the Ballarat goldfields, not related to sheep.

The Black Horse Quartz Company, a consortium of several experienced miners headed up by Edwin Witherden, had negotiated a sub-lease on some 600 feet of land within the Learmonth run in return for a royalty on any gold they found. With several stockbrokers on the company's directorate, the Black Horse was floated and with that news began to flow. Soon the entire Egerton Reef in the "Learmonth Run" was being worked profitably. Then the crowds arrived. Once again, the population of Egerton swelled.

The initial width of the Egerton reef was 50 feet at the surface narrowing to 20 feet at the bottom at a depth of only 350 feet, a modest depth in comparison to others that were surpassing 700 feet. At the time, it was a generally held belief that quartz reefs were "richer as they increase in depth and in addition to this that they are wider." This later proved incorrect, but as such it is not surprising that as the Egerton Reef narrowed going down it was often thought that the gold output would diminish and eventually run out. This was the case in early 1867 when the Learmonth brothers thought they had reached all the gold to be found. However, the Egerton reef was known for its unusual composition – large breaks in the veins were common.

In the spring of 1867, Thomas Learmonth decided to give the mine another shot before he returned to England. He employed William Thomas whom he had known from the days at the New Enterprise mine and William Bailey, an experienced miner from the Staffordshire Reef near Berringa. At the same time, Morgan Griffiths was appointed as underground manager. The news of the appointments drew favour with the mining community:

> Mount Egerton - We have much pleasure in recording what perseverance and skill in quartz mining may effect. The Mount Egerton Quartz Mining Company, the property of the Hon. T. Learmonth, MLC, after a successful working for thirteen years was considered about three months ago on its last legs; but luckily for Mr. Learmonth, he engaged the services of Mr. Bailey (formerly of the Staffordshire Reef) as chief manager, and Mr. W. Thomas (late manager of the New Enterprise Quartz Company, Ballarat, an old and experienced miner) as working manager and through their perseverance and skill the reef was again struck, and gave the magnificent yield of 305oz. for the fortnight's crushing. The reef is from twelve to twenty

feet wide, and gold is visible all over the face. (The Argus, 7 October 1867)

The mine was suddenly back in action and the Learmonths back in the black. Despite the actual gold output kept private, mining and more so the rumoured yields at Egerton were met with great interest by the press and created considerable excitement at The Corner. There was interest in expanding the area. In early 1869 Thomas Learmonth was reputedly offered £20,000 for just 600 feet of his 24-acre claim. He declined.

THE PUDDLING COMPANY

As miners, the Learmonth brothers had their fair share of time in the courts. Shortly after William Bailey and William Thomas took over as Mine Managers at Egerton and news of the gold yields spread, the Learmonth brothers became embroiled in a dispute with the small Mount Egerton Steam Puddling Company, a group of seven miners and shareholders working a small claim adjoining the Egerton Mine.

The Puddling Company argued that Learmonth's underground operations had encroached on their claim. William Bailey argued that the gold reef being worked by the Learmonths dipped away from the Puddling Company's claim. With this information, the Puddling Company offered to sell their claim to Thomas Learmonth for £400. He responded by authorising William Bailey to buy the Puddler's entire holding for £200. William Bailey now faced the dilemma of pleasing his employers but empowered only to pay half what was wanted. There was no room for negotiation and Bailey did his best to secure the deal by downplaying the value of the claim. Eventually, Thomas Learmonth agreed to pay the Puddlers the full £400 and put down a £20 deposit. However, not all of the Puddling Company members were content and soon after some returned to the claim, sank a shaft and found their reef. This resulted in a lawsuit between the Puddling Company and the Learmonths, the Puddlers claiming fraud on the part of the Learmonth's representative William Bailey. Bailey became by circumstance the meat in the sandwich. It was not, however, to be his first venture into the courts for this reason.

In court, the Puddling Company argued for the sale to be set aside. In defence the Learmonths argued that the reef was theirs, the claim having been legitimately sold to them for £400. In turn, they sought for the members of the Puddling Company to uphold their sale. In extended hearings, some four months later judgment was finally made in favour of the Learmonths and they celebrated by driving their diggings into the Puddling claim. They found a gold lode some 35 feet thick. William Bailey's actions added to the Learmonth's riches albeit possibly at the expense of his reputation. For the Learmonth brothers, the Puddling case had set the scene for later legal developments in relation to their Egerton interests.

In the 13 years to 1867 the Egerton area had yielded thousands of ounces of gold and had seen many claims and owners. In the early days the depths were not great, however, the gold output still gave respectable returns to those who persevered. A lack of water and the abysmal state of the roads in and out of Egerton continued to dog the diggings. In the early 1860s, it was thought the gold at Egerton had been fully worked out and the depths attained had yielded all that was to be got from the claims. At one point the area lay completely dormant and deserted. However, technological advances saw the arrival of steam engines that could pump water and allow diggings to depths hitherto unknown.

Because the Egerton mine was privately owned by the Learmonths for the greater part of the 1860s the exact amount of gold produced is not known, unlike the mines that were in the hands of shareholders where yields and dividends were published daily by the local press. In the years following the appointment of William Thomas, William Bailey, and Morgan Griffiths, however, the yields showed satisfactory improvement. After costs, the Learmonths took £66,000 of profit in the four years to 1871. In 1872, the profit dropped to just £1,000 and in 1873 to £4,000. Once again it appeared that the Egerton gold had run out. William Bailey asked for further investment in equipment but by then the Learmonths had other plans.

SCOTLAND BOUND

As the 1860s drew to a close the Learmonths had pressing matters in their Scottish homeland. Thomas Learmonth Senior had forged the new pastoral trading opportunities of Tasmania in the 1830s and collected substantial wealth along the way. Having fallen victim to the recession of the 1840s he was prompted to return to Scotland where in 1864 he took the helm of the sizeable Scottish estate of Park Hall in Stirlingshire. Park Hall was reputedly an ancestral family estate that had been lost years earlier in a land dispute and it was the Learmonth intention to try and regain it, which with wealth in hand they did. This left his sons John, Thomas, Somerville and Andrew to pursue their own interests in the colony. However, toward the end of the 1860s, the family's colonial days were beginning to lose favour over a return to Scotland. Thomas senior was aging and fragile and having just regained control of Park Hall it was possible that once again the family may lose their ancestral home. This prompted Thomas Learmonth junior to return to Scotland in the summer of 1868. Here he assumed control of Park Hall and eventual inheritance when his father died the following year. John Learmonth also returned to England in 1870 to practice medicine but died a year later. In that same year, Andrew Learmonth had also returned to England on a semi-permanent basis but was making regular visits to the Colony.

This left Somerville the only Learmonth brother to deal with the remains of the family interests in Australia including the Ercildoune homestead and the Egerton Goldmine. With further Land Act releases looming over the pastoral lands, including at one point the Egerton mine itself being erroneously included in the surveys for selection, and much of their grazing leases about to expire; with a lost father and brother the foundation of the Learmonth Australian estate was shaking. Further troubles ensued as Ballarat entered 1870 in the grip of an economic recession. Gold output had fallen drastically throughout the capital-starved mines. Land tax was imminent. Ballarat West was declared a city in 1870 and Ballarat East followed suit in 1872 bringing in a raft of new bureaucracy and regulation.

In July 1873, Somerville Learmonth announced he was leaving Australia for good to the dismay of the local Ballarat establishment. The following month the vast Ercildoune Estate was put up for auction in Melbourne. With only a few genuine bids it was passed in at its reserve of £9 per acre. A few days later it was privately purchased by Sir Samuel Wilson for reportedly £250,000 including more than 26,000 acres of land, machinery, nearly 1000 head of cattle and around 32,000 sheep. Other assets followed suit.

A week after the Ercildoune sale Somerville Learmonth accepted an offer for the Egerton mine and the following month, he left Ballarat for Sydney to deal with the family holdings further north. For the large part it seemed the glory days of the Learmonth brothers' pastoral pursuits in Ballarat, indeed Australia, were over. In their wake, they left a highly commendable legacy of building, pastoralism, enviable stock improvement and advances, and a reputation held in extremely high regard through all echelons of society and defining the stature, stamina and guts of the early Victorian pioneers. However, their Egerton story was not quite finished.

LEARMONTH VS. BAILEY

In 1871, the Egerton Mine generated a disappointing £1,000 profit reflecting the generally depressed state of gold production throughout the Victorian goldfields. Wanting to re-join his brothers back in Scotland, Somerville Learmonth decided to sell. He put its value at £50,000 and entrusted his manager William Bailey to find a buyer. Over the coming months Bailey canvassed potential buyers however in the midst of a recession, the investors were shy. When no buyer would touch it, Learmonth dropped the price to £40,000. Still there was no interest from either mine developers or the cash-poor mining investors. Over the following year, Bailey canvassed a price of £25,000 and then £20,000 but still no interest. Unwilling to improve the mine's prospects and commercial viability by investing in new machinery, Learmonth again dropped the price to £15,000. Based on the profit from the mine in 1872 rising to a still modest £4,000 this seemed like a more reasonable value. As the summer of 1873 approached and the shearing done, Ercildoune was sold in August. With time running out and his departure imminent, Learmonth pressed Bailey to broker a deal on the mine.

When news of the Ercildoune sale made the press, several suitors for the mine then came forward. Learmonth received an indication of interest from James Williamson, then manager of the Union Bank and Martin Loughlin, the wealthy Ballarat mining investor who wrote to him inquiring about price and terms. Learmonth told Bailey to speak with Loughlin and show him around the mine, which he did. Finally, in September 1873 and with the ink barely dry on the Ercildoune sale, Bailey presented Somerville Learmonth with an offer of £12,000 from Martin Loughlin. Learmonth countered saying that if Loughlin was willing to meet him halfway on the price, namely £13,500 he would accept. This Loughlin did and the deal was done. Loughlin was well known for never passing up good opportunities when it came to equity capital.

Two weeks later Learmonth summoned Bailey to Ercildoune and paid him his promised £700 commission. He thanked him for a job well done and said goodbye to the man that he had trusted in his employ for the previous seven years. It was in this scene that William Bailey in a heartfelt expression of emotion cried tears. This event later earned Bailey the nickname "Weeping William Bailey" and it is by this he became known to his dearest friends. The nickname remained with him for the rest of his life and into modern day folklore. A few weeks later Somerville Learmonth left Ballarat for Sydney.

With goodbyes done and the Victorian assets largely divested this seemed an appropriate point to end the fine legacy the Learmonths had established in Australia. However, two months later came the disturbing news: Somerville Learmonth filed a lawsuit against William Bailey and Martin Loughlin claiming conspiracy to defraud him out of the real value of the Egerton mine.

The mining community was astonished.

What transpired in Sydney that caused such an action is unclear other than to say that Learmonth may have acted on rumours that he had been swindled. He admitted that his brothers had been pressuring him to sell the mine but possibly they were disappointed with the final price. England at the time was giddy for investment opportunities in the Australian goldfields and a declaration that they had sold a valuable mine in Ballarat at any price may possibly have been met with embarrassment.

What transpired in Egerton after the sale was very clear. On taking possession of the mine in the weeks following the sale, Martin Loughlin immediately increased resources and focused efforts on that part of the mine that was in need of new equipment, equipment that the Learmonth brothers had in the light of their departure and intended sale of the mine, rightly declined to provide. With new resources, the mine's fortunes turned.

Two weeks later TC Thomas and four other miners were working underground on a drive in the Rose shaft of the Egerton mine. The shaft was at 300 feet below ground. As was the practice, the miners put in a "rise" from this level digging out poor quality stone but as they went up the stone got better. They then realised the reef was both above and below them. Soon good rock was being taken out and sent to the stampers. The rock yielded 60 to 70 ounces per ton. What TC Thomas had found was the latest and new gold rich vein of the fickle Egerton reef.

To Somerville Learmonth news of the gold find was met with bitterness. Upon his return to Ballarat, he was introduced to George Warren, a former magistrate and mining speculator from Melbourne. Warren had no actual mining experience and had never set foot on the Egerton claim however he had been a recent shareholder in the adjoining Black Horse mine which had not made him much money. Warren was not a wealthy man, admitting in court that he was worth maybe £1,000 but regardless of his means, he claimed to have expressed intentions to buy the Egerton mine for £25,000 prior to its sale to Loughlin. Upon introduction, he told Learmonth he thought the mine was worth £100,000 to £200,000 – a figure not based on any working knowledge of Egerton and certainly not reflecting the fact that he had just sold out of the adjoining Black Horse. In itself, Warren's stated intention to pay £25,000 for a mine he regarded worth more than quadruple his offer may well have been tantamount to a swindle – Martin Loughlin's intention was to on-sell the mine in London. With a lawsuit now in play, and despite being totally unknown to Somerville Learmonth, Warren was hired to gather evidence against Bailey, his payment to be £5,000 if the mine was recovered. Over the coming weeks, Warren played the part of the detective and snooped around the miners, the mine and the stockbroking community at The Corner. He found no evidence and reported such back to Learmonth, receiving just £40 for his efforts.

Regardless Learmonth pressed on with his lawsuit. He asked the court to set aside the sale and that ownership be returned to him. He claimed that William Bailey had "improperly worked the mine" in the months leading up to Loughlin's offer, in an effort to purposefully reduce the gold yield thereby inducing Learmonth to sell at a lower price. Bailey defended that he did not in any way degrade the yield intentionally and that he was unaware of Loughlin's intention to purchase until Somerville Learmonth informed him of the fact. Both agreed the gold yield following the sale had increased greatly but Bailey noted that so did the costs as new equipment was purchased by Loughlin. Learmonth also claimed that Bailey had conspired with Loughlin in a deal to become a shareholder in the mine.

The trial lasted several months in the Supreme Court with both sides retaining the finest silk representation money could buy. On each side, the best legal counsels argued in detail the events of the months of August through October 1873 and the intricate workings of the mine. Called to testify on what gold was found (and when) were many of the Egerton miners including TC Thomas and Morgan Griffiths for Bailey. The collusion claim heard refuting testimony from a number of the prominent stockbrokers and businessmen of Ballarat including Bailey's brother Thomas Bailey, Edward Morey, Owen Edwards, Martin Loughlin, Henry Morris and Robert Ditchburn. George Hathorn (the publican at Craig's Royal Hotel) was called to account for Loughlin's movements around the time of the sale. Testimony was given and refuted; there were accusations of jury tampering and missing evidence. The trial captured the public psyche like a gripping drama exposing the lives of their most respected citizens – the transcripts reported daily in the press and taking a fair amount of column space country-wide.

As the trial dragged on relations between the parties involved deteriorated. Accusations flew as evidence on both sides was gathered and heard, and even the miners at Egerton were split. At one point a fracas broke out in Egerton between William Bailey and one of the miners testifying for Learmonth, to the point where Bailey rose to anger and struck the miner, drawing blood. In response, the miner caught Bailey "by his long beard with one hand and a very tender part of the body with the other" and held him there until they were separated by some of the men who were spectators of the whole scene. The miner eventually let go taking with him a considerable portion of Bailey's beard.

It what may have been the worst insult to William Bailey, Learmonth concluded his court testimony saying that before hiring

Bailey they would have sold the mine for £1,000 but Bailey had yielded net £70,000 in profit and then added: "He might have got more gold if he had managed it properly." In light of the fact that Learmonth had kept William Bailey in a position of great importance and within his employ for at least seven years, it seems that Somerville Learmonth was suffering a great deal of seller's remorse salted with a liberal amount of bitterness. Although he admitted that he had not even been to the mine in more than nine months, in the six months prior to the sale Learmonth had yielded 2000 ounces of gold from Egerton under Bailey's watch. In the six months following it produced 10,000 ounces for Martin Loughlin. On the surface, it is easy to see why Learmonth concluded conspiracy. However, the Egerton mine had played with miners for more than three decades and such turnarounds were not unusual in its long history. In 1873, this particular turnaround was being officially tested.

Tired of Egerton and in the dusk of his mining days, William Bailey intended to retire following the sale. However, Loughlin intended to float the mine for £20,000 to London investors, recouping his own investment and making a profit on the way through. With all mines now valued based on not only their gold prospects but also the credibility of effective mine management, it was crucial to Loughlin that he retain a respected manager. He convinced Bailey to remain on as operating manager with an increased salary and a one-quarter equity share for which Bailey had to pay the sum of £2,000. To this Bailey agreed in the understanding that his tenure would only remain until such time as the enterprise was floated, anticipating this would take just a few months. Morgan Griffiths was also retained as the underground mining manager and for all intents, the Egerton Quartz Mining Company looked like a golden jewel – a proven deposit, effective management and a happy workforce. In fact, the township of Egerton generally celebrated as all of the resident miners retained work and a new spirit of hope and enthusiasm prevailed in the knowledge that the mine would survive and keep them gainfully employed.

After lengthy and detailed testimony, the case approached summation. It became clear to both Learmonth and his legal counsel that he had failed to prove his complaint. Before allowing the judge to rule, Learmonth abruptly withdrew his case.

However, a few weeks later a fresh suit was lodged by Learmonth and this time he petitioned not only Bailey and Loughlin but also Owen Edwards, James Williamson, Edward Brayton and William Davis as well as the entire Egerton Company. Owen Edwards was an independently wealthy mining investor and a sharebroker at The Corner. James Williamson was the manager of the Union Bank in Ballarat. Together Bailey, Loughlin, Edwards and Williamson were intended shareowners in the new Loughlin venture. Learmonth contended they were all party to the original deal and that Edwards and Williamson acted in collusion with Bailey and Loughlin. Brayton and Davis were later released from the complaint after the judge granted their objection to being parties to the claim.

At the same time, Learmonth also sought an injunction to restrain the mine from being worked and to have a receiver appointed. This was also refused much to the relief of the hundreds employed at Egerton. When Learmonth petitioned for the diggings to cease, which they did temporarily, alarm bells rang as it was heard that several parties had been hastily formed ready to jump the claim.

The only successful request made by Learmonth was to prevent Loughlin from floating the company and any of the four shareholders from selling any of their shares. The Court did agree to all derived profits being held in suspense at the Union Bank until such time as a verdict was found. All the while the mine continued to be worked with Loughlin and Edwards personally bankrolling the mines' expenses.

After months of deliberations, the Court eventually found in favour of Bailey, Loughlin, Edwards, and Williamson. In summing up, the Judge found that Bailey had actually done better in securing a sale price of £13,500 as he had been permissioned to sell at £12,000. He noted that Learmonth knew that it was Loughlin's intention to float the mine for just £20,000. He derided Learmonth for withdrawing his first suit and then using it as grounds for his second suit. He found that preventing Loughlin from dealing in shares would be to the severe detriment of the Ballarat mines, the compensation for which "could not be measured". In directing the jury, the Judge said that although there seemed reason enough to be suspicious, suspicion alone was not sufficient grounds to prove a complaint and that as plaintiff, the burden of proof rested with Learmonth. He told the jury they must determine their verdict based on the rules of evidence produced and that they could find independently on each issue. It took the jury just three hours to deliberate. Finding unanimously in favour of the defendants on each of the complaints made, the saga was finally over some two years after its commencement. The mining community was relieved.

In June 1876 at the Egerton Mine, Morgan Griffiths received a telegram announcing that on the final day of proceedings in Learmonth vs. Bailey the jury had found unanimously in favour of William Bailey. Immediately jubilation spread throughout Egerton. The whistles blew, the local band marched through the streets, followed by the mine workers, and flags flew on every post including those of neighbouring mines. The day was summed up in the local press with the following:

> The 13th day of June the word
> Came up with lightning speed
> To Egerton, that on their case
> The jury all agreed.
>
> The joyful news soon spread around,
> The cheers were long and loud,
> Their exultation clearly proved
> Of Bailey they were proud.
>
> The band turned out, played martial airs,
> The engine whistles blew,
> The stormy wind let loose, as if
> For Bailey and his crew.
>
> They praised the merits of the four,
> And drank their health with glee,
> They each of them received a round
> Of cheers - three times three.

> They lauded Trench, McDermott, Purves,
> And Holroyd for their skill;
> Such demonstration ne'er was seen
> Before upon the hill.

(The Bacchus Marsh Express, 8 July 1876)

Finally, the Great Egerton Mining lawsuit was over. About 140 Egerton miners were employed at the mine so the impact on the small close-knit community was considerable. Of those miners, only a few gave evidence for the Learmonth side and they were immediately ostracised. In January 1877, pending Somerville Learmonth's departure for the homeland, the Learmonth witnesses approached him in Melbourne asking that he make some provision for them as life in Egerton had become untenable. It is unknown if this request was ever met.

Despite the jury's unanimous agreement in favour of William Bailey and for all intents the case considered closed, Somerville Learmonth continued his pursuit by preparing to take an appeal to the Privy Council. However, six months later sanity prevailed. He finally conceded and agreed to drop his case with each party being responsible for their own costs. For the shareholders William Bailey, Martin Loughlin, Owen Edwards and James Williamson this amounted to a huge £26,000 combined, but for Somerville Learmonth it was a whopping £75,000 representing most of the profit he had derived from the mine since appointing Bailey and Thomas.

By the time the case was dropped the gold dug from the Egerton mine since its sale to Loughlin saw a profit of £146,000 - held in limbo at the Union Bank for some three years. But the real winners were the lawyers who made a tidy £100,000 plus without so much as digging a hole.

On a stifling hot day in December 1876, news that the case had finally been put to rest broke at The Corner. Celebrations at Craig's Royal Hotel let loose and champagne flowed in honour of William

Bailey, Martin Loughlin, Owen Edwards and James Williamson. Once again, the bands marched through the streets of Ballarat and flags flew. The turnout for trading at The Corner that day was described as "thin".

In the midst of the trials, Somerville Learmonth tried to buy back the Ercildoune homestead offering a premium of £15,000 over his original selling price. He was unsuccessful. Then in early January 1877, he left the colony for good and sailed home to England. However, obviously unperturbed by the whole episode, a month after the jury verdict came in, he quietly purchased a new gold claim at Elaine, just south of Mount Egerton. It was barely mentioned in the press.

Unable to inherit any of the Scottish estates due to the laws of primogeniture, but still with considerable wealth in hand, Somerville Learmonth retired to London where he died the following year at age 58.

The Learmonth foray into Egerton life was never going to be easy and to some extent, their path had been set well before the Great Egerton Mine lawsuit. Among the resident townsfolk of influence in Egerton included storekeeper Charles Foreman, the postmaster Edwin Witherden, storekeeper and businessman Ralph Wing Tanner, stockbroker and miner Henry Morris, stockbroker and miner Oliver Randell – all past partners in the Mount Egerton Steam Puddling Company whom the Learmonths had sued some years earlier for the opposing side of much the same reason.

Learmonth vs. Bailey presided in history as the greatest and most controversial mining case the colony had ever seen. It had enormous implications for the future of Australian mining. A verdict in favour of Learmonth may have well opened a floodgate of claims on other mines, mine owners, and mine investors and the effect may have rippled into other areas of commerce and industry. The verdict in favour of Bailey reiterated the fact that a deal once signed and delivered is not negotiable and that due diligence rests on the part of both buyers and sellers before the deal is sealed.

However, perhaps the greatest irony of Learmonth vs. Bailey was this: as Learmonth successfully blocked Loughlin's intended flotation of the Egerton Quartz Company on the London Stock Exchange for just £20,000, he also prevented the four shareholders from selling any of their shares during the term of the trial. The end result was that riches that were to follow at Egerton, particularly from the Sister Rose shaft, remained in the hands of Loughlin, Bailey, Edwards and Williamson. By default, it made them incredibly rich. The profits which would otherwise have been diverted to London investors or bound for Scotland actually remained in Ballarat. As Learmonth was asking for the return of ownership and not simply a greater sale price, and the men best positioned to exploit the mine he was presently suing, one is left to wonder what would have happened to the mine had Learmonth been successful in his complaint.

Over the following decades, the case of the Great Egerton Mine lawsuit made its way into the newspapers time and time again, especially as those involved died, and the period was recounted by various witnesses, onlookers and the like. It made good fodder for the columns. The stories got bigger as did the numbers.

While Learmonth and Bailey were polar opposites in Ballarat life - Learmonth an aristocratic young pastoralist and Bailey a brash young entrepreneur, the case polarised as old money versus new money and the journalistic slant depended on which side was taken.

THE QUARRY, THE ROSE AND THE SISTER ROSE

> It was among the earliest quartz discoveries in Victoria, was one of the richest mines ever worked, and was the subject of as protracted as well as one of the most expensive law proceedings that ever engaged the attention of the colonial courts. It is another example of the vicissitudes of gold exploration. For years thousands of ounces repaid the earlier proprietors, to be followed by a period of depression that led to the widespread belief of the mine having seen its best days. Then came a reaction, and with better gold than had ever been won, and anon further decline. And so it has been with this as with others, until by dogged perseverance a depth has been reached which places the future (so far as experience in other fields can foretell) beyond any reasonable doubt. (The Argus, 19 August 1885)

The Egerton mine comprised three main shafts. The first was the Quarry shaft on ground originally part owned by the Puddling Company. The extent of the gold found in the Quarry earned it the nickname "The Bank". It was said, "The gold carried the quartz instead of vice versa, and some of the pieces were so large that they were cut with a chisel and sold in that condition". By 1885, the Quarry had reached a depth of 900 feet encompassing 11 levels with payable stone throughout. The Quarry shaft was later taken up by the Black Horse Company, which worked it through to the 1890s.

The next was the Rose shaft, which was mined down to 700 feet over nine levels. At the time of the mine's sale to Loughlin, the depth of the Rose was nearing 300 feet or the third level, but the yields were mediocre, showing less than an ounce per ton. Further down the stone was as much as 50 feet wide but the yield dropped to just a half ounce per ton. However, as the shaft developed the stone was only eight feet wide in some places, in particular as the miners drove upwards from the third level back to the second level. But here the yields were as much as 60 ounces to the ton.

Although it was yields from the Rose shaft that caused the contention in Learmonth vs. Bailey, the greater Egerton riches were yet to come. In the midst of the lawsuit in 1875, another shaft was opened up about 500 feet to the north of the Rose shaft. It was called the Sister Rose and it was sunk down to 500 feet over seven levels. Stone produced from the Sister Rose once again saw the Egerton reef give up its golden riches. With all the shafts now opened, the supply of quartz was greater than the Egerton battery of 23 stampers could reduce so it was necessary to add another battery of 20 heads and a new smelting house.

Over the following years, work at both the Quarry and the Sister Rose continued to produce stunning yields, often finding stone up to 20 feet in width. In 1878 alone the Sister Rose produced 7,753 ounces of gold. By 1880, the yield had somewhat declined but still 40,000 tons produced just over 12,000 ounces. Similar results continued for some years with profits amounting to just over half of the total value of the gold obtained. In the 10 years following the Great Egerton Mine Lawsuit, more than £600,000 of gold was won from the Egerton Mine with shareholders receiving £282,000 in dividends and workers receiving around the same in wages. By the end of the century, the Rose shaft had been worked down to 800 feet, the Sister Rose down to 1,000 feet and the Quarry shaft was surpassing 1,700 feet below ground.

In the neighbouring Black Horse mine, drilling connected the shafts of the Quarry and the Rose. It was here that "perhaps the richest patch of golden quartz ever met with in the State was found." On the eastern side, in a V-shaped deposit known as "the indicator" was a layer of gold that measured about 60 feet in length, around seven feet wide and two feet in thickness, the whole of which was reportedly "hung together with gold". It alone contained £300,000 worth of gold.

In the 1890s, the Egerton Quartz Company and the Black Horse amalgamated. Together they were considered fine examples of mine management both economically and in terms of working practices. While accidents did happen, in the 30 years of workings up to 1885 only one miner had lost his life.

In 1903, a survey of the mines reported that the goldfield of Egerton had produced more than 25 tons (over 700,000 ounces) of gold in the 50 years since the first discovery, on land covering only 300 acres. While many of the Ballarat mines were by this time closed or worked out, the surveyor noted on Egerton "There is room here for a good rush or two… with well-applied effort, Egerton should have a successful future".

It was not to be. Despite the promising outlook, a year later the decline of Egerton had begun. A prolonged drought had severely impacted operations at the mines causing many miners to move on to find work in Melbourne and to new mines opening up in Western Australia. A newly negotiated wage arbitration award forced the drought-stricken Egerton mines into the red, alongside many of their Ballarat and Bendigo counterparts. With the increased expenses and little chance of profitability, capital investment stalled. It was reported, "Those interested in the industry were anxious to do the best they could for its welfare, but they felt that it would be a hard matter to induce the public to put their money into the mines with little prospect of any return." In the 12 months that followed, Egerton was practically deserted, shops were closed and 1904 saw the resumption of licences for five of the town's hotels with more to follow.

In the first week of December 1906, the famous Egerton Mine ceased operations. The manager was instructed to pull up the pumps and haul tram rails and equipment to the surface. By this time only three men were employed at the mine, and within a few days they also were out of work.

In 1918 the 80-foot-high chimney stack was demolished, its 25,000 bricks reclaimed for building use and by 1927, all that remained was a huge jumbled mullock heap and a portion of the stone engine pumping house. Belying its service to other great Egerton "wars" this old structure was later dismantled except for one end. It became a fitting memorial for the fallen young sons of Egerton miners who embarked for Europe to serve the allied forces in World War One.

Today Egerton resembles a tiny, quiet village on a road less travelled. Both peaceful and picturesque, its mining history is not instantly recognisable. Although not a part of the original mining operations, an old and decommissioned government gold battery sits proudly on a rise, in roughly the position of the former Black Horse Mine. The original Mechanics Institute Hall is preserved, as is the historic primary school. There are examples of original cottages still intact. A closer look reveals relics that echo the past – the rail tracks to the stamping house, occasional discarded parts of steam engines, and other mining tools that remain in-situ.

THE STORY OF
WILLIAM "WEEPING" BAILEY

Having come to Australia from England in 1848 William Bailey was one of Ballarat's "Old Colonists". He began his working life in Australia as station manager in the Amphitheatre district near Avoca but soon headed to the newly discovered goldfields in Bendigo where he worked as a digger on a claim in Eaglehawk Gully. Other early jobs included storekeeping and farming. In the 1860s, he became the manager at the Staffordshire Reef mine near Berringa before being hired as Mine Manager for the Learmonth brothers.

After the dust settled on the Learmonth court case, William Bailey continued on as chairman of the Egerton Quartz Mining Co, remaining in the position until 1883. When local shopkeeper Ralph Tanner was elected to the board, Bailey resigned his position in apparent disgust. However, this was not the end of his mining days. As Egerton brought him fame and friends in high places, his other purchases bought him fortune.

In 1879, he partnered again with Martin Loughlin to buy a 6,000-acre property from a bankrupt farmer for £36,000. It was called the Seven Hills Estate and covered some eight square miles of land around Kingston to the north of Ballarat and close to the rich goldfields of Creswick, Allendale, and Clunes. Over the 20 years from 1880 to 1900, the gold mines on Seven Hills became some of the area's most famous, yielding more than a million pounds of dividends for Bailey, Loughlin, and the other partners. All the while, with mining underground, they leased the surface to farmers thus deriving income that somewhat sheltered them from the mining busts. After the gold ran out in the late 1890s the property was subdivided and sold off as small farms, raising £55,000.

Bailey's interests extended into grazing when in 1884 he purchased a half share in "Terrinallum Station", a 47,000-acre pastoral property on the outskirts of Camperdown, south-west of Ballarat, paying the price of £230,000. His partner in Terrinallum was Agar Wynne, a wealthy pastoralist, and later politician and also the son of Edgar Wynne, an associate Bailey had been in business with since the late 1850s. The property was part of the estate of the late John Cumming MLC, a Scotsman from Aberdeen who like the Learmonths settled the land for the pastoral purpose of raising sheep. Neighbours included the Chirnside family (of Werribee Mansion fame) and the Manifold family, all early Victorian squatters. Not known for its gold deposits, Terrinallum became one of the finest sheep and cattle grazing properties in the district. At Bailey's death, his half share in Terrinallum was valued at £135,000. The station was eventually sold to Lindsay Nicholas, heir to the Aspro empire, and his wife Hephzibah Menuhin, an accomplished violinist and sister of the renowned violinist Yehudi Menuhin. During the 1940s, the station played host to many celebrities including Vivien Leigh and Sir Lawrence Olivier, and of course Yehudi Menuhin.

A common interest in the Bailey, Chirnside, and Manifold families was the love of thoroughbred sports. All were active in the early days of the Victorian horse racing circles and Turf Clubs. Also, noted for his keen interest and contribution to Victorian horse racing, William Bailey was widely respected amongst the upper echelons of the Victoria Racing community.

Despite his gold and pastoral properties stretching throughout central and western Victoria, William Bailey always stayed close to Ballarat. In 1883, he built his beloved "Bailey Mansion" at the corner of Mair and Drummond Streets. Italianate in style and resembling the grand Werribee Park mansion built by the Chirnside family, the mansion and its original gardens were a tribute to the death of his daughter who died of fever due to poor drainage associated with the site's original bluestone house. At one point the newly built mansion's external scrollwork was painted the colour of "Egerton Gold" to reflect the origins of his fame, perhaps in a humorous snub to his local detractors. After his death, for some years during the Great Depression, the Bailey Mansion sat empty due to exorbitantly high maintenance costs. Saved from demolition it is now a functional part of St John of God's Hospital. The mansion stands in a quiet mark of respect to the wealth exhumed from the heyday of the Ballarat Goldfields. It has been described as one of the most palatial homes west of Melbourne and to this day is an important Ballarat landmark. It is widely reputed that William Bailey's ghost walks its corridors.

In the autumn of 1906, at age 78 William Bailey died quietly at his mansion, the place in which he lived in retirement. His legacy amounted to just shy of £170,000 left to his wife and six children. At his death, he still owned shares in TC Thomas' South Birthday Mine at Berringa valued at £20.

THE STORY OF
OWEN EDWARDS

The youngest of twelve children, Owen Edward Edwards was born in 1828 in the shipbuilding city of Barmouth in West Wales. His father and namesake was Master Mariner Captain Owen Edwards, a highly respected sea captain who sailed the trade routes from England to the East Indies from the early 1800s. His mother Catherine was the publican of the Ships Inn in Barmouth for many years.

Having spent a few years in a seafaring life, Owen Edwards junior arrived in Ballarat in 1852, a carpenter and sailmaker by trade. He set up shop in a building on Main Road in what was then downtown Ballarat, opposite the Charlie Napier Hotel. With partners William and John Davies, their business "Edwards and Davies – Tent and Tarpaulin makers" operated successfully throughout the 1850s and well into the late 1860s satisfying the needs of the constant stream of miners making their way to the gold fields.

The business flourished and provided financial security allowing Owen Edwards to return to Wales in 1856 where he married his childhood sweetheart Catherine Hughes. Upon their return to Ballarat together they set about having a family, bearing four children all up but sadly losing three sons in early childhood. Funeral notices for the lost sons reveal the family was living at the corner of Humffray Street and Main Road in Ballarat, likely the same premises used for the tent business.

By the end of the 1860s, Ballarat was fast on its way to becoming a metropolis and the requirement for tents and tarpaulins abated making way for permanent housing and more stately buildings. As such Owen Edwards closed shop and let his premises to a draper and tailor. With much of the gold mining activity in Central Victoria now corporatised, the late 1860s saw Owen Edwards emerge as a stockbroker and mining agent at The Corner. It is known that Owen Edwards was an investor in many of the major mining companies in the area including the prolific Prince of Wales Quartz Mining Company and he was noted for being "in most of the good things" in the early days. His stock portfolio was impressive; however, some bad investments and poor timing saw him go bust on several occasions.

The rest of the 1870s and through the 1880s saw him regain his wealth and his position heightened by several directorships taken in Ballarat mining ventures. In 1886, the Prince of Wales and Bonshaw mine in Sebastopol was reopened as a corporate venture. The directors were William Bailey, Owen Edwards, Morgan Griffiths (the Egerton Mine Manager), Edward Morey (a later Ballarat Mayor and fellow broker) and Peter Matthews (a pioneer of steam pumping and puddling gear). In the late 1880s, the official Ballarat Stock Exchange came into being and Owen Edwards became one of its founding members.

Following the financial collapse of the 1890s, Owen Edwards again fell on hard times. Whilst he was still socially respected and held in high esteem he did not resort to charity or financial welfare. To avoid destitution, he worked as an errand boy at the Mining Exchange and was in charge of ringing the bell signalling the open and close of trade.

As a respected member of the Ballarat community, Owen Edwards was known for his civic disposition and generosity. His philanthropy included donations to various church groups, the Creswick Mine Disaster Fund and many other charities and needy. He was a committee member of the Ballarat Benevolent Asylum and past president, likewise the Ballarat District Hospital. He was also a founding member of the Old Colonists Association and had an active role in the formation of the Mechanics Institute. In 1877, he was made a Justice of the Peace and in this capacity presided over a number of magisterial inquiries in the district over the following decade. He is also known as a committee member and one of the chief originators of the Welsh Eisteddfod in Ballarat.

His early sailing roots were never far from his heart and his sporting pursuits were most noted in yachting where he personally owned several craft, often sailing to victory in regattas on Lake

Wendouree. He was the first Commodore of the Ballarat Yacht Club, one of the founding members of Colac Yacht Club and was known for funding the various activities of both from his own pocket. The Ballarat Yacht Club was largely the domain of the Ballarat stockbrokers and many of the members were active in the sport. It was reported that during one particularly dry year in Ballarat, water in Lake Wendouree had fallen to such a level that racing activities were threatened. Despairing, the brokers convinced the owners of the nearby Lady of the Lake mine to pump water from the mine into the lake. At the rate of two million gallons per week, the water level was raised to launch smaller boats. Then a welcome week of heavy rain restored the lake back to boating levels and racing resumed.

Several years after the death of his wife Catherine, Owen Edwards remarried at age 75 to Mary Thompson, the widow of a former Ballarat Mayor. However, the following year, after a prolonged illness that saw Owen Edwards retire from public positions, he died quietly at his home in Lydiard Street. Once one of the wealthiest men in Ballarat and of considerable fame, his death was widely reported in newspapers throughout the country:

> Mr. Edwards' declining years were spent in comfort.
> The deceased was of a very bright and cheerful
> disposition, and his death has removed one of the
> leading figures in the mining history of Ballarat.
> (Kalgoorlie Western Argus, 19 December 1905)

Flags in Ballarat were flown at half-mast in tribute to his passing.

If not for two significant events Owen Edwards may have fallen into history being remembered only for his stockbroking days and civic activities in Ballarat. His first splash into the public arena came with his involvement in the famed Learmonth vs. Bailey Egerton mining case where he was a partner in the consortium with William Bailey and Martin Loughlin. Having secured a quarter shareholding in Loughlin's new Egerton Quartz Mining Company, Owen Edwards was to broker the float of the new enterprise on the London Stock Exchange.

The second and possibly more notable event is his association with the iconic Eureka Flag.

A EUREKA STORY

The Southern Cross flag used by Peter Lalor to swear in the diggers at Ballarat's 1854 Eureka Rebellion is ingrained in Australian culture as the symbol of a free nation. In its 160-year evolution, it is widely considered to be the peoples' icon of unity, its appearance signalling the birth of a free democracy. But its origins have forever been shrouded in mystery, folklore, and subjective speculation. Who made it and why the Southern Cross? Over time, these questions have proposed some interesting solutions.

Popular culture has it that the flag used at the Stockade was sewn by miners' wives Anastasia Hayes, Anastasia Withers and Anne Duke in a goldfields tent. However, a recent re-creation of an undertaking in the magnitude required to make such a flag has largely debunked this theory. Other hypotheses include taking designs thought up by a Canadian miner present at the rebellion, others suggest the flag drew influence from ecclesiastical references and also other existing flags. There is also some evidence to suggest the flag design originated in Tasmania and was first displayed there some three years before the Stockade.

First public mention of Owen Edwards and the Eureka flag came in July 1899 following the death of Mr. William A.G. Fraser, a Ballarat school teacher. In reporting his death, the Ballarat Courier cited Mr. Fraser as "the maker and hoister of the flag that flew above the Eureka Stockade". However, the following day saw this claim refuted in a letter to The Courier from respected Ballarat historian William B. Withers. Withers had for some time been trying to determine the authenticity of a specific Southern Cross flag held at the Ballarat Art Gallery. In his letter, he stated that he had interviewed Fraser about the flag a year earlier but found that Fraser was unable to identify it. Withers also questioned Fraser's widow Elizabeth Fraser who said she found The Courier's claim surprising as her late husband had previously made no mention of it. In short Withers dismissed the Fraser claim outright stating "I may say that your informant is not right" and that the claim was "too remarkable to be regarded as reconcilable with the acceptance of your informant's statement as credible." Therein the story of Fraser and the flag should have stopped although some still assign his name to the undertaking. The Courier's claim though prompted Owen Edwards to weigh in.

In the days following, Edwards said: "there appears to be a misunderstanding of the matter." Further:

> Mr. Edwards claims to have been the maker of the Flag, and says the work was executed at his tent shop in the Main Road. Three flags were made for the diggers by Mr. Edwards and his partner, the late Mr. Davis [sic Davies]. Mr. Edwards states he has good reason to remember the stockade flag, as the insurgents, in the subsequent excitement, forgot to pay for it. (Town Talk, Geelong Advertiser, 1 August 1899)

This statement raises interesting conundrums in the popularised Eureka Flag story. It has long been thought that only one flag was made for the Reform League and that its tattered remains are today carefully housed in a purpose-built Ballarat museum dedicated to its preservation. It also appears that, unlike Fraser, Withers made no comment to the contrary on Edwards' claim.

The notion of the flag as a commercial commission by the Ballarat Reform League is somewhat supported by a newspaper article that appeared shortly after the conclusion of the Eureka Rebellion trials. In January 1855, following the sedition trial of Henry Seekamp (the editor and owner of the Ballarat Times), the Geelong Advertiser and Intelligencer reported on Seekamp's conviction and six months imprisonment sentence:

> Great stress has been laid on the "Australian Flag;" this is hardly fair; the origin of this flag was this: — At the various meetings which were held on Bakery Hill, each nation had its flag as may be seen from the reports of

> these meetings at the time: thus the Union Jack, the Stars and Stripes, the Tri-colour, and the flags of Ireland, Scotland, and Germany were placed around the platform. On one or two occasions considerable ill-feeling arose from the national desire to have each of these flags on high poles, yet with all their rivalry on this point, the Union Jack was highest in every instance; this does not indicate a very rebellious spirit; however, to prevent all squabbling, the Committee determined to have a flag, a simple one to be called the Australian, under which the whole community might meet to consider public matters. There was nothing very warlike about the flag, the one belonging to the Anti-Convict League, might with far more justice have been objected to, though such was not the case. (Geelong Advertiser and Intelligencer, 27 January 1855)

Further mystery is added by reports of the flag's location over time. In 1891, upon the death of John Basson Humffray, obituaries mention the flag as being in the possession of the Museum of the Melbourne Public Library. This was again repeated in 1893 upon the death of Peter Lalor. However, the following year saw another remarkable claim:

> Mr. Archibald, of Warrnambool, writes to The Argus that the flag erected on the Eureka Stockade by the miners is in the possession of Mr. James King, Minyip, Wimmera, having been taken down from the flagstaff in the stockade after the fight by his father, the late Mr. John King, at that time in the police service, and who afterwards lived in Warrnambool. Some strips were torn from it, and there are bullet holes in it. It is otherwise in fair order, and was for some time in the possession of the late Mr. P. H. Smith, inspecting superintendent of police, who returned it to Mr. King, in whose family it has remained ever since, Mr. Archibald evidently wants to get that flag for his public museum in Warrnambool to put alongside Louis Napoleon's 1848 baton. (The Australasian, 29 December 1894)

The claim made by Owen Edwards in 1899 may otherwise provide intriguing information to deepen the already murky waters of the Eureka Flag mythology. However, in 1905, his death notices saw the claim widely repeated.

> Mr. Edwards, who was a sail maker, was entrusted with the manufacture of the Southern Cross flag, under which Peter Lalor swore in his men preparatory to the encounter at the stockade. (The Age, 11 December 1905)

Whilst the concept of Owen Edwards being the maker of the flag is probably not quite as romantic as today's popularised stories, it is certainly not without merit. He was known to be in the vicinity of the meetings of the Reform League (Charlie Napier Hotel) at the time of the Rebellion. As a sailmaker, he had the skills and materials available. He had known associations with both John B. Humffray and Charles Dyte (a fellow sharebroker), both key players in the Eureka Rebellion among others. Also, given the flag became so contentious following the rebellion there was good reason to keep quiet about its origins.

As to the design, it is possible to reflect that influence may have been drawn by the Southern Cross constellation which, by no coincidence, was and is the mariner's main celestial navigation tool for charting waters to Australia - a nautical fact that would have been familiar ground for Owen Edwards.

CAPTAIN MOONLITE
AND OTHER OUTLAWS

At Egerton, there were a few who sought to get the gold by means other than digging. In May of 1869 Andrew Scott daringly robbed the Egerton branch of the London Chartered Bank. Taking nearly £700 in cash and a cache of gold from the Egerton Mine workings worth around £500, Scott then penned a note signing it as "Captain Moonlite" before taking flight.

Irish-born, Scott arrived in Australia just a year earlier. He claimed to have served in the Maori Wars of New Zealand, but this was not the full extent of his supposed military history. Along with New Zealand, he also claimed to have joined the famous freedom fighter Giuseppe Garibaldi in the Italian War of Independence and also claimed to have served in the American Civil War, however, there are overlaps in the dates thereby discounting one or more of the claims. It is generally accepted that he was present in the goldfields of the Californian gold rush prior to coming to Australia.

His father was an Irish clergyman who had expected his son to follow suit, but instead, Scott studied engineering. Arriving in Bacchus Marsh, Scott opened an office as a civil engineer, but his religious familiarity landed him the role as a lay preacher in Egerton, which was desperate for some form of religious instruction and worship. Finding the miners' attitude to him unresponsive and wanting to satisfy an apparent grandiose want of respect, Scott then made a bold if not uncharacteristic move on obtaining his own fortune.

Approaching the London Chartered Bank after dark, he came across the bank's young agent Ludwig Bruun. Pointing a pistol into Bruun's back he said: "Don't make a sound or you're a dead man." But Bruun immediately recognised Scott's voice and laughed, to which Scott responded with "Don't laugh, you bloody fool. Open the door and get inside quickly."

After relieving the bank of its Egerton gold treasure, Scott then forced Bruun to the local school to write a signed note stating that Bruun had "done everything in his power to withstand intrusion". He then made his escape.

Scott headed to Sydney where his grand war stories gained him entry into society. With his newly acquired wealth, he pretended to be a squatter, which opened all the right doors into Sydney's glitterati. He sold his gold at the Sydney mint and purchased a yacht which he intended to sail to Fiji. This was to be his undoing after the cheque used to pay for the yacht bounced. He was then apprehended for the crime of uttering just before he and his yacht sailed past Sydney Heads.

Spending the next two years in jail for the cheque charge, at one point he faked insanity in order to secure release. This got him a few months in a lunatic asylum.

Meanwhile back in Egerton, Bruun and another were charged with the robbery. In a bizarre moment, Andrew Scott was called as a witness in Bruun's trial, refuting Bruun's claim that he, Andrew Scott, was indeed Captain Moonlite. The police believed Scott and dismissed him but later found insufficient evidence to convict Bruun.

Scott was released from his Sydney jail in 1872 but was immediately re-arrested in connection with the Egerton robbery. The police had finally worked out that Scott's testimony during Bruun's case was a ruse and he was sent to Ballarat for trial. Whilst awaiting his court date Scott escaped from the new Ballarat jail, fleeing to Bendigo where he was eventually again apprehended.

The following years saw Scott in and out of prison, all the while still trying to satisfy his want of fame. In 1879 he built himself a gang – mainly made up of misguided youths, some as young as 15 - and with them set out on a trail of bushranging. Ending up in New South Wales, Scott, and his gang corralled several hostages at a station near Wagga Wagga while they held up various businesses in the town. At each outing, more hostages were taken and before long the group was so large in number that Scott could no longer control them. One of them escaped and managed to alert the police. In a standoff at the homestead, Scott escaped again, this time with police in hot pursuit. Later at another homestead Scott and his gang were finally bailed up, amidst a gun battle which resulted in the death of the youngest of Scott's cohorts. Scott surrendered with his bushranging gang, two of whom later died from their wounds, and Scott was taken to Sydney for trial. In January of 1880 Andrew Scott, or Captain Moonlite, was found guilty and was later hanged at the Darlinghurst gallows.

Of all the notorious Australian bushrangers, Andrew Scott was perhaps the most misguided. Most of the outlaws had some justifiable reasons for their actions – poverty, injustice or persecution. Scott had none of these. He had been a simple preacher in the respectable and flourishing community of Egerton. He held a well-paid job and had many friends.

Scott was neither the first nor the last of the robbers at Egerton, but he was certainly the most daring and notorious. In 1882, another attempt to rob the township of its golden cache came when £1300 worth of gold was stolen from the office of the Egerton Mine manager Morgan Griffiths. Within 15 minutes of the robbery, Griffiths raised the alarm and both troops and miners converged on the town like an inland tsunami. The police were still warm to the botched Captain Moonlite affair and the Egerton miners took the event personally, likening Egerton gold to be their own. Later that night the would-be robber was intercepted by townsfolk as he was leaving Egerton on horseback. However, his stolen cache was so heavy that he dropped it as he was leaving town. The gold recovered, no names were ever attached to the would-be thief who absconded away into the night, several pounds lighter.

A pub, The Corner and politics

EGERTON REGROUPS

On Wednesday last a gentleman from Ballarat visited Mount Egerton. He had passed over a parched and burnt-up country all the way, when suddenly, just as he entered Egerton, down fell some heavy drops of rain. Anon a heavy pour commenced, such as the Egertonians had eagerly been longing for. The Ballarat visitor found himself in the midst of a lot of buoyant people, and was himself in high glee when he saw, with his own eyes, that the quartz crushing companies' dams were being rapidly filled. He had no carrier-pigeon, but he had a horse, and hurriedly putting on the harness, he drove back with all speed to Ballarat. As he neared the town, the scene offered new delights. He found the roads as dry as he had left them. In and around Ballarat not a drop of rain had fallen. Now for his chance. Off he posted to one of our sharebrokers. 'Buy me some shares in the Black Horse,' quoth he. 'The price is so-and-so; you can give a little more but buy them.' 'I cannot get them at the price,' says the broker. They have advanced during the day. At three o'clock it was known that rain had fallen at Egerton, and the shares advanced £.7 in price. 'At three o'clock', cried the would-be buyer, ' why the rain did not fall for fully half an hour after that!' And in truth this was the fact, but our Corner men had seen dark clouds hovering in the direction of Egerton, and commenced to speculate in Black Horse shares on the suspicion that the company's dam would be full of water. And they were right. (The Argus, 23 February 1869.)

The later 1870s saw the Egerton mining men turn their attention to other endeavours. With Learmonth vs. Bailey over and both the Egerton Quartz Mine and the Black Horse Mine steadily producing gold, the miners and townsfolk settled into daily life, raising families and growing the town. More children were born in the 1870s in Egerton than in any other period.

William Bailey stayed on as chairman of the Egerton Quartz Mining Company, married a local girl and raised children. He also partnered with Martin Loughlin to purchase a share in the Seven Hills Estate, which over the following decade produced more than 440,000 ounces of gold worth nearly two million pounds for its six partners. The mines in the estate included the Madame Berry, Lone Hand, Loughlin, West Ristori and Lord Harry – all prolific in terms of production and many continuing on through the turn of the century.

Morgan Griffiths stayed on as manager of the Egerton Quartz Mining Company until 1877 when he resigned in order to take an extended holiday back to Wales, taking up mine management at the Prince of Wales and Bonshaw at Sebastopol upon his return. Owen Edwards returned to Ballarat and continued his business of stock broking and speculative investing.

After a decade of gold mining at Egerton, TC Thomas had made a small fortune in some of his own mining claims including the Gordon and Egerton Company which he formed with Morgan Griffiths. He had also made many investments including shares in the successful Koh-i-Noor mines and the Black Horse mine, both of which were actively producing gold and paying dividends. A keen share speculator, TC Thomas partnered with Edwin Witherden in a share broking business at The Corner which ran successfully until Witherden retired. Therein TC continued on in his own right, acting primarily as a mining agent and investor.

In the 1870s release of Crown land, TC purchased a 20-acre farmlet on the outskirts of Egerton. This he used to raise horses for new racing interests. He also purchased a block in town situated on the main street of Egerton, conveniently located in front of what is now the historic government-owned gold battery. On this block, he built a hotel to serve the ever-growing need for good lodgings in Egerton. He named it the "Royal Stock Exchange Hotel". It was a lavishly appointed building and included an underground cellar. The cellar was often used for coronial inquests as it was the coldest place in town to store the recently deceased. The hotel closed in 1903 when licences were resumed by the government however it remained standing until at least the 1920s, possibly the eventual victim of fire or just dereliction. None of it now remains bar possibly the cellar as its only archaeological remnant.

By 1880 the township had 1300 permanent residents; a reliable water supply was being addressed, a Mechanics Institute built; clubs had been formed such as the Egerton and Gordon Racing Club and Rifle Club (complete with a state of the art 1000 yard range), both of which had TC Thomas on their directorate.

Roads were still a problem, in particular the road between Egerton and Gordon which was dangerous at best but impassable in the wet. This was a major issue for the Egerton mines and in 1876 a deputation led by Edwin Witherden, Morgan Griffiths, and shopkeeper Ralph Tanner petitioned the Buninyong Shire Council, which had jurisdiction over part of Egerton, to make the roads good. While their request was well received, they were told there were not enough funds available for the area for the road to be metal surfaced. This was not the first time the council had denied spending – the debate had raged since the early 1870s.

To counter the impasse with the Buninyong Shire, several of the group stood for council on the neighbouring Ballan Shire. TC Thomas secured his vote and took the position of Returning Officer for West Riding; Edwin Witherden was already a councillor of long standing. The first order of the day was to consider a petition signed by 53 of Gordon's ratepayers asking for the district to be annexed under the Ballan Shire and in due course this proceeded. Incumbents installed, the road issue was dealt with and the problem finally resolved.

TC Thomas's tenure at the Council only lasted a few years and he opted out of re-contesting the following election. While his time at the Ballan Shire was a small dip in political waters, his wider family was making a much bigger wave back in his Welsh homeland.

THE STORY OF WILLIAM MABON ABRAHAM

TC Thomas's uncle was a man by the name of William Abraham although he was more widely known by his bardic name of "William Mabon Abraham" or just "Mabon".

Like TC, Mabon grew up in the Welsh coal mines, his father a working collier and copper smelter. Raised in relative poverty and with minimal education, like many of the Welsh miners he started work in the coal pits at age 10. In his 30s, Mabon found a greater calling when he was appointed a miners agent and later rose to the position of vice-president of the Monmouthshire and South Wales Conciliation Board.

He rose to fame in a controversial election in 1885 after he reformed the Cambrian Miner's Association, building the union membership from nothing to 100,000 strong. With the support of the miners behind him, he won the election for the new Rhondda Division of South Wales securing 56 percent of the vote. From there he played a prominent role in the miners' struggle which led to the agreement for drawing up a sliding scale of wages in the Welsh coalfields in relation to prices and profits. He was the miners' chairman of the Joint Sliding Scale Association until it was terminated in 1903. From 1892 to 1898 the South Wales miners did not work on the first Monday of each month, a scheme to limit output in order to maintain wages. This was known as 'Mabon's Monday'.

Sitting in the House of Commons from 1895 to 1918, Mabon was also the first president of the South Wales Miners' Federation and treasurer of the Miners' Federation of Great Britain. He was made a Privy Councillor in 1914.

As Mabon was also widely recognised in Australia, many of his principles formed the basis of Australian mining practice and conditions for working miners. In the mid-1890s, he received an invitation from Australia to come to the Colony and act as an official labour arbiter with an annual salary of £2000. This he declined. In England, he was offered a Knighthood by Queen Victoria which he also declined – twice.

The Right Hon. William "Mabon" Abraham died in Wales in 1922 at age 79. While still today being heralded in Wales as the "Miner's hero" and a champion of the Welsh working classes, it was upon his death that controversy raged following the revelation that he had on his political journey amassed a fortune, much to the chagrin of his support base. Due to his respect extending to Australia, especially among the mining community and union organisations, his death was widely reported in the Australian press:

> William Abraham (Mabon), the veteran Welsh Labor leader, who recently died at the age of 79, left a fortune of £33,315 (writes a London correspondent). As Abraham commenced his life's work at the age of 10 in a Welsh coal-pit, the worth of his estate was a surprise to everyone. At one time Mabon was in great request as a public speaker and received good fees, but this did not account for the £33,000. Mr. Abraham also drew royalties on the sale of a sauce to which he "lent his name". When Mabon retired from the leadership of the Miners' Federation he received a gift of £5,000. The real source of William Abraham's fortune however, was a chance investment of £400 in a Welsh industrial business. During the war this concern paid substantial amounts into its reserve funds that at the end Mabon's share amounted to £19,000. Abraham was also a director of a Scottish insurance society first merged in the London Edinburgh, and Glasgow Co and later with the Pearl Assurance Co. When the amalgamation came about, the Labor leader received a good bonus upon his shares and compensation for the loss of his directorship. In fact, Mabon is an excellent example of a Labor leader who "made good". Genial, honest, hard headed and hardworking he deserved all he got.
> (Western Star and Roma Advertiser, 18 November 1922)

THE STORY OF
EDWIN WITHERDEN

Of all the miners of Egerton, Edwin Witherden possibly had the longest and most varied association with the mount. Born in Kent, England and the son of a corn dealer, he served an apprenticeship as a carpenter before leaving England in 1851 bound for New York. He was just 20 years-old. However, a new life in America was not to be and he returned to England soon after where his adventurous spirit saw him once again set sail to join the rush of miners to the new goldfields in Australia. Arriving in Geelong in 1853 and then trekking north to Creswick, over the next year he followed the rushes from Creswick to Talbot, Dunolly, Castlemaine and Stawell before finally arriving at Egerton shortly before the Eureka Stockade.

At Egerton, he partnered up with David Syme (later founder of The Age newspaper in Melbourne), Henry Wyatt and Oliver Randell (both later members of the Ballarat Stock Exchange) and others to work the quartz deposits on the mount. Their small prospecting party pioneered the Egerton goldfield over the following years; however, their equipment was rudimentary and quartz crushing at Gordon was an expensive business. Often the party only made enough from their digs to feed themselves.

The Eureka Stockade created many fugitives as the authorities hunted down for trial those they deemed responsible for inciting the melee. Two of the insurgents who found themselves on the run were Frederick Vern and Charles Black, both close associates of Peter Lalor. In the aftermath of the Ballarat riot, Vern and Black fled to Mount Egerton – the reward for their arrest set at £500 each. Finding refuge and shelter within Witherden's party, the pair narrowly missed capture when they were passed off to the pursuing constabulary as recently arrived relatives. Witherden was a staunch supporter of Peter Lalor, and their friendship remained throughout their lives. He often hosted functions for Lalor in Egerton during Lalor's later life as a politician.

In the early 1860s, when the gold at Egerton was thought to be worked out, Witherden headed north to Queensland and was one of the first miners in the rush to new gold at Charters Towers, but the Queensland ventures disappointed and like many other hopefuls he soon returned to the digs at Egerton which by this time had found new favour. As the Egerton Quartz Mine gathered pace, Witherden leased a small block from the Learmonth brothers and set up the Black Horse Mine which he named after his homeland's Kentish Coat of Arms. It was to become one of the most productive mines in the area, lasting into the turn of the century and considered exemplary of good mine management.

While mining made Witherden rich, his later pursuits included running one of the local stores and the post office in Egerton with his brother-in-law Charles Foreman. In the day, the local store was not only the hub of the community, but it was often the place where out-of-luck miners would trade their mining rights for provisions. This probably led to Witherden's association with The Corner in Ballarat where he took up share trading in the 1870s, later as a principal in a broking firm and mining agency with TC Thomas. Like TC, Witherden was also one of the founding members of the Ballarat Stock Exchange.

Witherden's entrepreneurial bent extended beyond that of gold mining. In the 1870s, he exploited one of the unique characteristics of the Egerton area. From its earliest records, the land surrounding Egerton was densely forested but also largely covered in the native hop bush known locally to the indigenous as "Sticky Hop". The drought-tolerant bush was a favoured food for the immense kangaroo population as well as being used in traditional indigenous medicine and weapon making. But the most common use for the plant in the advent of the gold rush was its fermentation into the second most in demand product after gold – beer. Being a hop, the plant was a natural contender for exploitation by the miners who made it one of their staples. Often, beer was the beverage of choice especially when drinking water supplies were either putrid or non-existent. With demand high and the plant known for its ability to withstand very dry conditions, Witherden seized the opportunity to cultivate an extensive hop field on his property called "Kent Villa". His crop became known as one of the finest in Australia and for many years, he dominated the local hop growing business with great success. However, a grasshopper plague put an end to his famous hop crops and he took up farming livestock, dairy, and food staples like potatoes and kaffir limes. Today in a much-diminished industry, hops for brewing are grown largely in Tasmania with some varieties grown near Mortlake in Western Victoria. Today, native hop is often considered a weed with environmentalists advocating control of this once useful and abundant plant.

In the 1880s, Witherden went on to become a Justice of the Peace and Ballan Shire Councillor and also one of Victoria's early magistrates. Following retirement, he furthered his farming pursuits in Gippsland before retiring to Melbourne. From his humble beginnings as a miner to activities including stockbroking, farming, and politics, Witherden represents a true colonial entrepreneur. At his death, he was described as being always of a happy jocular disposition, and fond of sport even when well up in years, his favourite pastimes being cricket and shooting. He died in Melbourne in 1915 at age 84 and is interred at the Ballarat Cemetery.

BENEVOLENCE

> It is a startling and melancholy fact that amid all the boasted wealth of the goldfields, and the numerous openings and rewards which are there supposed to be within the reach of every industrious man, there should exist numerous instances of real and unmitigated distress, amounting, in many cases, to utter destitution.
> (The Star, Ballarat, 2 December 1857)

Success on the Ballarat goldfields was not assured, and many went home none the richer or indeed penniless often having spent their entire wealth in pursuit of gold. For those who did achieve success, their position was generally not held in ignorance of those less fortunate. This is very true of the sharebrokers, investors, and managers – those who did well out of the precious metal – with many of them being actively concerned with the welfare of those to whom the goldfields were not kind.

In 1857 the Ballarat Benevolent Association was formed to assist the "distressed, orphaned or deserted" and many of the names at The Corner were either active in administration or contribution to the fund with many of them leaving large bequests to the various charitable institutions upon their death. The 1870s saw the formation of the Old Colonists Association of Ballarat which sought to provide relief for the early miners who had fallen on hard times – again many of the investment community members were founders and active and charitable. Along with the Ballarat Club, the Old Colonists Association has a proud history of benevolence, charity, and philanthropy. Both continue to provide support to this day, with the building erected to house the latter a prominent Ballarat historical landmark.

Mining accidents were common throughout the Ballarat goldfields and many miners lost their lives in pursuit of gold. As the mines moved away from singular "diggers" trying their luck and into corporatised ventures with the backing of capital provided by investors, the mine extents grew rapidly and the depths passed 1000 feet. At this depth, the water was known to be hot enough to boil eggs and the air quality exceedingly poor. In the early days, the resultant labyrinth of tunnels threatened to destabilise the geoscape of Ballarat itself and reports of building subsidence in the main business areas caused by the underground activities were a major concern. Within the mines themselves, reports of shaft collapses, machinery failures, and explosions litter the newspapers of the period.

Possibly the worst underground accident occurred in 1882 in Creswick, 20 kilometres north of Ballarat. The workings of the New Australasian Mine ran adjacent to the abandoned shafts of the original Australasian Mine. A misreading of the position of the old shafts and a subsequent wall collapse saw the new shaft inundated and 40 miners were trapped underground amid rising water. Thirteen managed to escape unharmed and only five were rescued – 22 miners lost their lives. The accident enraged the local communities and 4000 miners marched with the funeral procession of the dead to the Creswick cemetery.

Following the accident the Victorian Mining Accident Relief Fund was established and the community generously donated to raise money to aid the families affected by the disaster. Many large donations were received from the speculators and investors at The Corner as well as the wealthy mine managers and owners and within a few weeks, the fund had grown to £25,000. A compulsory levy was placed on all the Ballarat Exchange members without objection.

In the case of the Creswick widows, a few chose to use their benefits to sue the owners and management of the mine, much to the annoyance of the investing community. It appears the fund initially established to help just the widows was slow in dispersing benefits and its purpose extended to provide relief for all mining accidents, not just the Creswick widows. The fund paid compensation for almost 50 years, providing relief to any miner permanently disabled by mine accident and their dependent relatives anywhere in Victoria. However, the legacy left by the Creswick accident was to see the implementation of compensatory support to the miners whose lives were daily put at risk in the goldfields. It also led to significant advances in mine safety throughout the late 1800s and well into the early 1900s. The fund is also perhaps the earliest Victorian example of a worker's compensation scheme.

FEME COVERT

> A young and beautiful actress, a young and affectionate husband, a young and amorous manager. These are the parties to a big divorce suit now about to come on. They are all well-known people, and society which has gossiped a great deal about the marital arrangements of the parties is all agog for the disclosures expected. Certainly there is any amount of dirty linen to air, but the dirt is of the old kind. (Camperdown Chronicle, 28 February 1885)

Women in the Ballarat goldfields in 1854 numbered a little over 4000 compared to 12,000 men. Many wives were left at home in England and Europe while their husbands came in search of gold. Some brave wives sailed out to join their husbands in the years to follow.

In the early days, a woman's life in the goldfields was difficult, offering only the most basic of life necessities. In many cases, even that was wanting. The home was usually just basic shelter consisting of a tent with rudimentary fittings, no running water, no sanitation and very little in the way of comforts. Food had to be hunted, foraged and grown. Often the women were left alone to fend for themselves while their mining husbands worked in faraway mines, or alternatively, the home had to be mobile as they rushed around to new gold finds. Some women worked alongside their husbands panning in the creeks and shallows but as mining went underground women were relegated to the camps to keep the home fires burning.

Children posed additional challenges. Without basic medical services such as doctors or midwives, childbirth was usually assisted by female friends where available or alone where not, often with horrifying repercussions. Goldfield graveyards are littered with stillbirths, infant deaths and in some cases the death of the mother herself. Where children did make it past infancy, there was little in the way of education and nothing in the way of child services including medical assistance. The children made do with whatever playthings they could find, often in and around mining equipment. With no such thing as child care services, mothers were tasked with keeping the home in order as well as an eye on the kids for every waking hour of every single day.

Of the women fortunate enough to live close to a township, even one that was still evolving, some relief came in the form of general trade. As the mines matured and more men settled for regular paid work, so did a wife's ability to settle and raise her family in a proper home, with actual walls and doors. The merchants servicing the mines brought with them goods and chattels, the growing populace attracted doctors and shopkeepers and news from home was easier to come by. The women formed their own little communities, protecting each other when husbands were away and supporting each other in raising their families. Often staying within their own, almost every township and miner's camp had its own little nationality-based enclaves. The British stayed with the British, the Irish with the Irish, the Welsh with the Welsh, the Chinese with the Chinese, and so on.

More than 95 percent of the 4000 females in the Ballarat gold fields were married women. This came with more sinister disadvantages. Under English common law the Rules of Primogeniture governed the inheritance of estates whereby only male sons (or nephews) were able to inherit land from deceased estates. For married women the inability to inherit was further exacerbated by the Laws of Coverture. Under colonial rule coverture for women applied in Victoria for most of the 19th century.

There were two distinct types of women under the Laws of Coverture. A "feme sole" was an unmarried woman who was legally recognised in her own right. She could conduct affairs on roughly the same basis as men, buy land and stocks and enter into contracts. Then there was a "feme covert". She was a married woman. The laws stated that upon marriage a woman gave up her entire legal identity. This meant that she was unable to own property in her own name and unable to enter into contracts in her own right. She was, in essence, non-existent in terms of the law, being "civilly dead", and her reason for being purely in servitude to her husband. The law assumed that the last contract a woman could ever enter was the contract of marriage. Under the thin veil of "unity" a husband and wife were regarded as one entity and, in all cases and circumstances, the husband was considered the dominant partner.

The Laws of Coverture also determined that upon marriage any property (including personal possessions) owned by a woman at the time of the marriage automatically became the controlled property of her husband. This included any inherited property, beneficial interests, or income earned by her before and during the marriage. The husband was free to do with the property and income whatever he wanted without her consent. The net effect of coverture was that a married woman was unable to accumulate wealth in her own right and she had to give up any independent wealth she had before marriage.

Overall the law guaranteed that very few if any, married women held any position of authority or power on the Victorian goldfields. Unable to buy land, unable to buy stocks, unable to take office, unable to borrow money and certainly unable to reap the gold rewards in their own right, married women were at the bottom of the fiscal ladder in all respects. This left them extremely vulnerable, more so than single women.

In terms of married life, an unfaithful, unhappy or abusive marriage saw women trapped within the confines of the laws of coverture. In the earliest days, a marriage could only be dissolved if a woman could prove numerous cases of adultery by her husband. It was a serious matter involving public court hearings at a huge cost. For wives of the more prominent Ballarat men a divorce case was considered of enough significance for its proceedings to be reported in the daily press and often the details were salaciously posed as scandal. For many unhappily married women, without independent financial means, a divorce almost always led to social ruin. The court was not compelled to rule a financial settlement between the couple. Violence, neglect, and desertion were not grounds for divorce until near the end of the century. Of those who braved escaping a bad marriage without divorce, many faced utter destitution. Many ended up in brothels or running "sly grog" shops in order to get by. In Ballarat, the Chinese community took in many homeless married women including their children. In itself, this fact was frowned upon by the wider community and led to the women being further ostracised and demonised.

A deserted wife was by no means safe. With no financial support from a husband, any income she earned by her own means was fair game for her husband's creditors. Her only recourse was to seek a "protection order", again involving a public court hearing wherein she had to prove her husband had left, unlikely to return, and not within reach of the judiciary.

The other way a marriage was dissolved was by death. If a woman's husband died, then her civil rights were restored. However, this was rarely a financial boon for widows on the goldfields. Upon death, a husband's wealth and assets did not (and legally could not) automatically pass to the wife. There was no recognition of her as the sole survivor. Instead, it passed according to the husband's last will or in the case of no will to the husband's deemed heirs, which often included children, brothers, sisters and parents. This left widows in the same position as if they were still married. Further, a widow who chose to re-marry was then subject again to coverture wherein all of her possessions passed to her new husband. This reason alone saw many men reluctant to Will their wealth to their wives.

Everything changed in 1882 when Victoria passed new laws under the banner of the Married Women's Property Act. With these new laws, for the first time, a married woman's civil rights were essentially the same as an unmarried woman. She could buy property, buy stocks, earn and save income and inherit in her own right. For many of the early Ballarat wives, the legislation came too late. By the time it was passed, the free land selections had finished, the heyday of the gold mines was nearing an end and all the public positions were well and truly entrenched with men. Consequently, there are no recorded female stockbrokers or politicians in Ballarat throughout the 1800s.

The Act, while it legally restored rights, did nothing to compel society to accept or make good the rights of married women. Most men, from a wealth point of view, still regarded wives with deep suspicion, if not complete disregard.

And then there was still the issue of death. The Act was not retrospective nor did married women gain any leverage in assets already owned by their husbands. As such many widows saw their "husband's fortune", often including their family homes, sold out from under them, dispersed to the husband's creditors and distributed to the wider family.

The Ballarat gold rush, indeed, the Australian gold rush, was thereby almost exclusively to the benefit of men. Examples in the fiscal plight of married women can be seen in many of the deceased estates of Ballarat's most notable men.

For example, many husbands left their wives just a small amount of money (£200 being the maximum allowed by coverture) and possibly an annuity. Many a man directed that all of his real estate be sold, and proceeds distributed to his wider family. This often left the wives in the desperate position of having to buy back family assets, including the family home.

In some cases, wives were "permitted" by a Will to remain in the family home until say the youngest child came of age or until she decided to move or until she died. Whilst this kept some widows and their children in comfortable circumstances, at no point did she inherit any real property. Testaments of this type are common in content to many of the stockbrokers of the Ballarat Stock Exchange and indeed many of Ballarat's wealthiest businessmen and public figures.

As an example of the devastating effects of coverture, TC Thomas' sister Tabitha was caught by the transition from pre to post the Married Women's Property Act. When her husband Morgan Griffiths died unexpectedly in 1889, he left no will. She inherited nothing. Seeking to continue her life and raise her children Tabitha was granted administration of his £4,000 estate only after paying a court ordered bond of £4,000. As a married woman and despite having spent her life at the forefront of the richest of the Ballarat gold mines, Tabitha had no money of her own. She had no assets and she probably could not borrow from the banks who generally viewed women as financially irresponsible. However, Tabitha was one of the fortunate few. Morgan's friends William Bailey and James Williamson came to her aid, putting up the bond and allowing her to take control of Morgan's estate.

At the time, Tabitha had six children in her care ranging from age twenty down to age eight, including one that was disabled. Eight years after Morgan's death, her children decided to sue her for not having sold the assets of the estate and distribute to them their share. This was a dilemma faced by many widows. In short Tabitha received a one-seventh share of her "husband's assets". However, somehow she had to educate, clothe, feed and shelter her children until such time as they could fend for themselves.

Tabitha's administration of Morgan's estate, in which every move had to be agreed by both Bailey and Williamson, saw her retain control of Morgan's real estate interests, from which she derived income to provide for her children, and his other financial assets such as shares - albeit in the midst of the worst financial crisis Australia had ever witnessed. This left her and the children in a comfortable position, especially as the estate held shares in Bailey's highly profitable mines at Seven Hills. The children received a good education, the family home was well kept and included household servants and Tabitha retained her social standing.

When the children sued their mother neither Bailey nor Williamson could be held responsible despite for all intents having the quasi-role of court-appointed executors. Bailey tried to defend Tabitha in attesting that the children had been well cared and provided for but against his advice Tabitha chose not to defend. As such the court upheld the children's petition and Tabitha's eldest daughter took over the administration of Morgan's estate including the bond put up by Bailey and Williamson. The assets were sold and dispersed, and Tabitha was now both homeless and stripped of many of her marital possessions.

Fortunately, she bounced back, taking up work with her brother TC Thomas in his new gold mining venture at Berringa and shortly before her death in 1912 she managed to purchase for herself a home in Ballarat held in her own name.

The turbulent 1890s

GIVE ME LAND, LOTS OF LAND

> As a rule there was a paddock somewhere which had to be bought, and a company or a "bank" had to be floated to buy the paddock. (Table Talk, Melbourne 21 December 1888)

Australia experienced its first great financial crisis in the early 1890s. As with all crises of this type it usually follows a great and over extended boom. The end of the 1880s was marked by a slowdown in Victorian gold production with the simultaneous increase in production of silver in New South Wales. Silver was cheaper to mine, and yields were more consistent. In short, silver was the new gold, and everyone wanted in. Money flooded out of Ballarat at breakneck speed. Places bearing silver deposits like Broken Hill in far west New South Wales showed the most promise. The Broken Hill Proprietary Company was formed as were many other silver ventures.

Around the same time, America was artificially enhancing the price of silver in order to bolster its own economy which was also coming out of a gold mining boom. Trying to force the adoption of silver as a standard over or alongside gold, America encouraged European countries to use silver as a form of security and currency exchange. Like Australia, America had plenty of silver but was also running out of gold.

In anticipation of silver leading a new boom and generating a similar effect on the Colony's finances and population to that of the gold boom, Melbourne set about an ambitious public works program. To fund works, vast tracts of land in and around Melbourne were made available for development. With the experience of the land deals made in the Duffy Land Acts still fresh, the speculators saw an opportunity in a new land boom and before long syndicates were formed to buy pockets of Melbourne real estate for development and resale. The banks got involved, discovering they could lend money to the land speculators based on the underlying wealth of the investors rather than the value of the real property being mortgaged. A bubble had formed.

The first sign that all was not good came when international talks over the adoption of a Silver Standard collapsed. America, which had amassed a silver stockpile, suddenly stopped buying and the ricochet effect was profound. The artificially inflated silver price began to falter, the silver mining market crumbled, and investors lost heavily. In just a few short years a considerable amount of the private wealth accumulated on the Victorian goldfields was lost.

At the same time, the about-face in inflated commodity markets collided with a fall in both wheat and wool prices - both Australian staples. Victoria's farming sector had been enjoying a wave of increased production but decreased wool and wheat exports resulted in farm layoffs. With unemployment rising, lower agricultural exports depleted the Colonial reserves and the boom stalled. Soon public works in Melbourne came to a standstill resulting in more layoffs. The building trades ground to a halt. The overextended banks faltered. The share market collapsed leaving many investors encumbered with silver and bank stocks that were now worthless - their cash locked up in speculative land investments for which there were no buyers.

With little money coming in, the Victorian Government needed to finance interest payments on its public works debt, so it turned to Britain. However, Britain had its own financial problems stemming from the collapse of Baring Bros a year earlier - the result of excessive and risky investments in Argentinian silver markets. Consequently, Britain virtually stopped all lending to the colony. By the start of 1891 Australia, indeed the world, was on the verge of financial collapse.

Before long the Melbourne land syndicates started to unravel, and questions started to be asked. Bogus land "banks" were discovered as was balance sheet doctoring by the major banks. Unable to raise money overseas the government sought to raise taxation which infuriated the labour force. In order to deal with the large number of company failures and shareholders suing for compensation, the government then passed a hasty law in the form of the Voluntary Liquidation Act. This enabled the crippled companies, many of them banks, to wind up for a fraction of their value thus giving shareholders an exit but no recourse on their investment other than the liquidated value. In many cases, that value was zero. For the investors, the prospect of holding for the longer term or until calm had been restored was immediately removed. Soon the Courts were overflowing with voluntary liquidations. Exacerbating events, the government then removed the courts from oversight of the asset sales, causing a freefall in land prices. Overnight buyers deserted the market. This included the wealthy British investors who had been long-time providers of equity capital.

In late 1891 most of the Victorian banks, or those that were still liquid, shut their doors in fear of a run on deposits. They also stopped paying interest completely. For weeks on end the banks remained closed, tying up an estimated £55 million of depositor funds. Many never re-opened. All the while the Victorian government continued its land sales.

Having never witnessed a financial collapse of such magnitude and exacerbated at every turn by seemingly kneejerk reactions of government, the investing community was stunned into silence. Unable to settle transactions due to bank closures, trading at the Melbourne Stock Exchange all but ceased. Many brokers went to the wall. A few returned to the Exchanges at Ballarat and Bendigo.

THE PRINCIPAL LOSSES

> The progress of Melbourne is marvellous. Eighteen months or two years ago a seat in the Stock Exchange of Melbourne was worth about £20. Today it is worth a £1000, the number of members being limited, and the last seat having been sold for £800. This is advance with a vengeance. Fifteen months ago a second minor exchange was formed, called the Melbourne Stock Exchange. This was initiated at £5 a member. Last week two new members were installed at £50 each. One doesn't require to invest in mining shares to make a fortune, a few shares in the two Exchanges would have been a very nice thing indeed. (Melbourne Punch, 8 September 1887)

With the opening of the new Ballarat Mining Exchange in 1888 and a similar one proposed in Melbourne, the future for Ballarat mining looked bright. By 1890, many of the Ballarat brokers had taken up seats on the Stock Exchange of Melbourne and moved their central business dealings to the state capital. While gold mining in Ballarat was still humming along, gold stocks were no longer the star performers. If the Ballarat brokers made fortunes in the gold rush, the events of 1891 certainly blew fortunes to the wind.

Having amassed enormous personal wealth, for some brokers their day to day share dealings had moved beyond dealing with the public paying small percentage commissions on share transactions. Possibly the only remaining providers of capital, many brokers were now acting solely as principal to the upper end of the investment market including wealthy investors and indeed government. Rather than acting as just the middleman between buyers and sellers they personally became the counterparty when large parcels of shares had to be moved, giving rise to the higher risk activity of "principal trading". They provided valuable market liquidity on tap in both start-ups and mature enterprises. They were also the first port of call whenever you had to float a company to raise capital to buy or develop something. While the new private Victorian "land banks" were springing up everywhere and silver stocks such as The Broken Hill Proprietary Company came into being, the Victorian Government also lent on the Ballarat principals to invest in the new public works enterprises such as the Melbourne Tramway and Omnibus Company and the Melbourne Gas Company.

The financial shock of 1891 hit the Ballarat brokers hard. Heavily invested in the Melbourne real estate syndicates and public works, the silver companies also made up a large part of their books. To stem their losses from the financial collapse the brokers became inventive. Many commenced to short sell – the act of selling shares you don't own in anticipation of a price fall - the intent to buy the shares back later at a lower price. When this practice was revealed (and reviled) the government tried to intervene. At the height of the collapse new legislation was proposed in the form of the Broker Licencing Bill. Again, it was kneejerk and ill-prepared. Under the veil of protecting the public from fraudulent dealings, most of which the banks were responsible for and had little to do with the brokers, the Act sought to outlaw short selling. The cash-strapped brokers were horrified. They faced having to buy back their short positions with no access to credit and no means of divesting other assets to pay for it. Condemnation was widespread and the Act was hastily withdrawn.

Instead, the government instigated a stamp duty on all sales of non-mining stocks, to be payable by the principal. This they thought would shore up the beleaguered bank stocks in the misguided belief that the practice would stop. However, neither of these happened. The banks continued to fall, and short selling became common practice.

Two of the most widely held shares in Ballarat were the new Melbourne Tramway and Omnibus Company and The Broken Hill Proprietary Company. In 1891 both had halved in value. By the start of 1892 bank shares were classed as unsaleable. Shares in silver mines were all but dead. The banks were calling in their overdrafts and the market was still in decline.

THE STORY OF BENJAMIN FINK

Perhaps the most telling story of the 1891 crash was that of Benjamin Fink, an original member of the Ballarat Stock Exchange.

Born in Guernsey, Fink was the eldest of nine children, his father a shipping merchant involved with trade between England and Australia which eventually led to the family's emigration to Victoria in 1860.

Well educated, Fink had displayed early financial acumen, a successful businessman running a furniture company in Melbourne. In the 1880s he ventured into mining, purchasing a financially stressed coal mining company in New South Wales and some pastoral areas in that state under similar conditions. In Victoria, he took up gold claims on the Majorca Lead and Duke Company in Maryborough. Both mines had largely been abandoned but Fink invested much needed new capital. His partners included William Bailey, Edward Morey, Alexander Lowenstein, Matthew Williams and Edwin Witherden. Within a year both mines were back in production, yielding an average of 1,500 ounces of gold per week and employing hundreds of miners. In Ballarat, he raised £100,000 and launched the Joint Stock Bank which he later merged into another of his enterprises, the City of Melbourne Bank, with many of the Ballarat brokers its main investors. This entity then became Victoria's largest buyer of gold from the mines.

As he rose in status both commercially and socially, he polled for the seat of Maryborough as an independent in the Victorian Lower House and won the election easily. In this position, he actively lobbied for legislative matters relating to mining to emanate from those actually involved in mining rather than non-mining politicians. This made him very popular within the mining community but made him very few friends in Melbourne political circles.

His first foray into Melbourne real estate was when he purchased several buildings at the corner of Elizabeth and Flinders Streets in Melbourne. The original owner of the lot was unknown, and Fink purchased the titles via adverse possession. All he had to do was occupy the buildings for a certain time after which he secured the titles for just £150 per foot of street frontage. The practice, known as "squatting", was essentially the same means as the original squatters secured their Australian pastoral estates. Using the equity in the buildings Fink then set about borrowing to buy more real estate, finding the banks eager to do business in the property lending market. Before long he had amassed a large property portfolio of premium buildings in the Melbourne central business district. If he could not buy a lease on a building or the building itself, he bought land and built on it. Many of Melbourne's finest buildings have their origins in Fink's portfolio, including the historic and iconic Block Arcade. His rental income was enormous, and the banks viewed him a premium client. In the lead up to the property boom, Fink became Chairman of the Mercantile Finance and Guarantee Company which in turn became one of the largest of the speculators in the Melbourne property market.

Another land opportunist was James Munro who was also one of the largest speculators in the "land rush" and owned several rival land banks. Munro was also then the Victorian State Premier.

The 1891 crash unravelled the commodities, agricultural, property and stock markets simultaneously. Due solely to the land crisis, it buckled Benjamin Fink. In the space of three years, his net worth fell from millions to near zero as the property and share markets crashed. Unable to sell its speculative property, the value of which was now plummeting, the Mercantile Finance venture failed, leaving debts of over a £1.5million.

Premier James Munro was also virtually wiped out by the land crisis he had helped to create. His land banks failed, leaving debts of just under £1million. About to be declared bankrupt he secured himself a prime government position in London, quit his position as Premier and sailed to England, to the outrage of the Victorian public. Replacing Munro as head of the government was William Shiels, a conservative liberal who the public prayed would return the state coffers back to more reconcilable values. But with the markets still in decline, the silver price still falling and the financially beleaguered Britain still reluctant to lend, Shiels could make no more headway than his predecessor. Failing to immediately address the problem of the land collapse, Shiels response was to cut government spending and introduce new taxes. As such confidence in Shiels also plummeted.

By the end of 1892, 143 Victorian companies had filed for bankruptcy and £35 million had been wiped off the value of the stock market, over ten percent of which was in silver stocks alone. As the financial crisis continued to deepen under his watch, and with bank failures starting to make daily headlines, Shiels tried to defer blame. With Munro gone, in his sights were the large land speculators still left in-situ, including one Benjamin Fink.

Unlike some of the land boomers who went bust and fled, Fink faced his debts publicly. At a meeting in September 1892 his various creditors agreed to settle his debts at the rate of half a penny in the pound (although a year later many of them tried to have the composition overturned). While the government was loud in its condemnation of the land boomers, Benjamin Fink appeared for all intents to have evaded total ruin.

Although it seemed the Shiels government had found its scapegoat, the calm that followed Fink's insolvency was very short lived. In early 1893 the American economy collapsed as the silver bubble burst, sending 500 American banks bust and a further 15,000 companies to the wall. By then the Australian recession was being called a depression. Shiels was ousted from office and the markets continued to decline. Creditor banks that had made early settlements with their bankrupt borrowers remained deluged by further insolvencies as the complexities of the financing system involved in the land crisis were revealed.

The crash of the early 1890s continued to weigh on the Victorian economy through until 1897 when both the American and British economies began to recover. By this time Benjamin Fink had moved to London. It was later revealed he had transferred a large portion of his assets to his wife thus preventing total loss. This mechanism was afforded to him only by the introduction of the Married Women's Property Act in 1882. Ironically, the champion of this Act through the parliament a decade earlier was none other than former state premier and Fink nemesis, William Shiels.

Accounts of the rise and fall of Benjamin Fink varied widely in the press of the day and show divergent views of both condemnation and praise. It is by no coincidence that Fink's younger brother Theodore Fink was then chairman of the Melbourne daily, the Herald and Weekly Times while the main supporter of William Shiels, and by all accounts the main reason for him being in office in the first place, was David Syme - then owner of the rival newspaper, The Age.

THE RESILIENCE OF
THE BALLARAT MINES

As the financial woes of Melbourne continued to wreak havoc on the State of Victoria in 1892 and 1893, the mining industry actually expanded. Gold production at both the Ballarat and Bendigo mines increased as did the shareholder dividends and both showed a return to production levels equivalent to before the land boom. Attributable to the fact that most of the companies on its lists were gold miners, stocks on the Ballarat Exchange rose in aggregate value. Many of the brokers who had left for the Melbourne Stock Exchange returned to their Ballarat and Bendigo roots and membership at both exchanges increased.

In Ballarat, TC Thomas, and his partner Edwin Witherden had weathered the storm of the depression and business at their Ballarat brokerage was brisk. However, like many of the other stock brokers, their principal trading activities saw losses, and many of their traditional clients had borne the brunt of the Melbourne collapse. Martin Loughlin, the biggest of the Ballarat investors, lost an estimated one-third of his wealth in property and finance deals and large investments in Melbourne infrastructure companies such as the Melbourne Tramway and Omnibus. Owen Edwards all but lost everything.

While gold was resilient, the culprit was silver. The brokers' books were laden with a debris of silver stocks now rendered worthless. An extended drought and a disastrous 18-week-long miners' strike at Broken Hill exacerbated the situation.

The biggest threat, however, came from the Victorian Government, which throughout the melee continually sought to stem the crisis through the introduction of new laws and taxes that targeted stocks and the stockbrokers with almost unrelenting fervour. This period saw the introduction of stamp duty on share sales and a tax on shareholder dividends. The latter was met with wide condemnation as the companies that were paying dividends were already taxed on their profits so in effect the tax was a double charge on shareholders. It would take almost 100 years to redress that standard when the "double dip" was abolished in the 1980s in favour of franked tax credits. Further exacerbating matters was the allowance of the beleaguered banks to withhold current accounts thus effectively locking up the monies the brokers were owed and ensuring that buyers were unable to complete their transactions. The various trust companies were released from their obligation to pay calls on partly paid shares, leaving the brokers with more worthless scrip as many of the prospecting companies failed through capital starvation. As the responsibility witch hunt continued in Melbourne, a proposal that the names of all shareholders in banks be publicly divulged caused many investors to depart the market for good. This particularly affected the principal traders who feared a future backlash if their positions became public.

On several occasions, the Munro ministry tried to pass the Licenced Brokers Bill which sought introduction of a number of new laws. It proposed that brokers should be licenced (fee to be paid to the government) and recommended a raft of new reporting requirements as well as the outlawing of short selling. The net effect of the bill would have been to practically legislate the Bendigo, Ballarat, and Melbourne Stock Exchanges out of existence - at a time when they were most under pressure.

At the same time, new mining markets were opening in Western Australia. The effect was to drain more capital out of the Victorian mines, far away from the silver mines of New South Wales and out of the reach of the Victorian Government.

The Ajax and the Birthday

BERRINGA

The latter half of the 1890s left the Ballarat stockbroking community down but not out. While maintaining his brokerage at the Ballarat Mining Exchange, TC Thomas turned his attention back to mine investment. In Egerton operations were still humming along with both the Egerton Quartz and Black Horse Mines still showing good output. His shareholdings in both kept books in the black. Next on TC's gold radar was Berringa.

Berringa lies to the west of Ballarat on the road south from Smythesdale. Several hamlets had evolved since the early days of shallow mining and the surrounding hills were scattered with small mining camps. The tiny township of Berringa was the central hub of life for the local miners. Prospected and worked since the early days of the rush, the area was known for its gold bearing deposits and many miners did well. Included in their number was William Bailey who cut his gold mining teeth at the nearby Staffordshire Reef. Although accurate amounts from the wider field in the early days were poorly recorded, the Staffordshire Reef reputedly yielded as much as ten tons (around 300,000 ounces) of gold at shallow levels.

From Smythesdale to Rokewood the shallow nature of these diggings was typical with most gold coming from just wash dirt and shallow shafts. The mining population was itinerant with many only staying for a brief period, often making just enough for the passage home or gaining enough experience to secure a pass into the bigger and more industrialised mines of Ballarat. For many years, a small Chinese community made an adequate living re-working the Berringa tailings and small deposits missed by the early miners.

For the larger part of the gold rush Berringa and its surrounds had a poor reputation. The biggest problem was a layer of granite that ran extensively through the area. To the early miners, without boring equipment, the granite was impenetrable. Not long into the rush the area was largely dismissed and there it remained well into the 1880s by which time most of the early miners had left, the remains of the mine shafts filled with water and the scant equipment fell into disrepair. Some of the early groups included the Long Thought of Company and Mac's Lucky which had some success but in general, a decent yield from the field was believed to be so unlikely that even the most hardened of the mining investors shunned the idea of prospecting.

The Berringa field had an unusual underground makeup. Its peculiar fracturing and seemingly endless granite layers both capped the treasures below and made it difficult to find and track quartz veins when the caps broke. Combine this with the inability to attract capital for many years and certainly in the heyday of Ballarat mining, Berringa was forgotten and for all intents deserted.

Then two things happened that were set to catapult Berringa back into the mining headlines.

In mid-1897 a young miner named David Le Page found the cap of the "Birthday Lode", named for the day of its discovery being the Queen's Birthday. On the heels of the capital drain, money to explore the deposit was extremely hard to find and despite securing a lease, Le Page struggled to get anyone interested in investing capital in the much-maligned area. Then in 1898, he found the only ones willing to take the risk. At the mining exchange in Ballarat, he joined forces with brokers TC Thomas, Robert Ditchburn, and Thomas Stoddart – all experienced mining men. Shortly thereafter the Birthday Company was formed with its head office registered at Craig's Royal Hotel and TC Thomas taking up the position of chairman.

The second crucial component also came with TC Thomas and party – the working knowledge of the fundamental transformer of hard to get gold deposits - dynamite. Just what you needed when the only thing standing between you and a wall of gold was a wall of rock.

Capital bought new equipment including a battery and stampers, steam engines and blasting tools. TC's sister Tabitha Griffiths took up residence in Berringa to oversee operations and his son Arthur Egerton Thomas worked the engine room. Fellow brokers also joined TC

Thomas in the development including Robert Bryant, an experienced manager from the Egerton mine. Labour was easy to secure with many of the Ballarat mines now closing. Before long the Birthday mine was producing gold and yielded 1,500 ounces from the first four crushings alone. Within months, the party commenced opening the bordering William's Fancy, the Kangaroo, the South Birthday and other mines following the extensions of the Birthday Reef. Over the next few years, as the granite layers yielded, the once maligned Berringa goldfield became the darling of the mining market. Once again TC Thomas had struck gold.

From its revival in 1898 through to its closure in 1918, the Birthday Reef at Berringa produced more than 160,000 ounces of gold, with the original Birthday mine alone taking out more than 73,000 ounces on a capital outlay of just £2,500. The Birthday Company never made any additional calls on capital beyond the investor's initial outlay, and it never failed to pay a dividend.

The Victorian Geological Survey reported the closure of the Birthday Tunnel and William's Fancy as "regrettable" and the likelihood of further finds as high. By the time of its closure, Berringa had deteriorated "from a prosperous village into a score of unoccupied homes".

Historically, the Birthday Reef combined with the adjacent Staffordshire Reef ranks as the ninth largest gold deposit in Victoria ever with an estimated 960,000 ounces of gold won on ground covering little more than a few hundred acres. A recent revival has seen gold once again being mined at Berringa, largely owned by foreign interests.

DAYLESFORD

As TC Thomas basked in the Birthday celebration his next venture was also to find similar fame. To the north of Ballarat lay the gold-rich area of Daylesford and the previously worked but now forgotten Ajax and Nuggetty gold reefs. Both reefs had been worked in the very early days of the rush but like Berringa had long since been deserted.

In 1899, a syndicate was formed called the Daylesford Mines Proprietary holding three abandoned claims at Daylesford, namely The Rising Star, Specimen Hill and the Nuggetty Ajax. The intention of the group was to rework these claims using modern methods. A lot of stone had already been unearthed but had been discarded as practically without value. The 1870s had seen the reefs worked with payable results down to about 800 feet.

The mines encompassing the three claims ran over 185 acres with a creek skirting one boundary and a range bordering another. In the Rising Star, the ground was mixed with slate and became poor as it entered a thick band of sandstone, the length of the gold-bearing portion or chute at the deepest workings varied in thickness from two to 25 feet. The Specimen Hill line of the reef was narrow and crossed by a railway line. Here it had a large formation which had in the past yielded rich returns from both surface and shallow depths. The Nuggetty Ajax covered an area of about 60 acres and contained three lines of reefs known as the Western, the Nuggetty, and the Welcome. All three had been worked with poor and primitive equipment and although the yields throughout were good, they were abandoned as soon as water became troublesome. The tailings and the contained pyrites had been allowed to run down to the creek, which for a while found favour with the Chinese who made decent returns on re-working.

Of the claims held in the syndicate, Specimen Hill looked the most promising as it had historically yielded well and was considered the easiest to re-open.

To fund working capital the Daylesford syndicate went to London, however, it took some time to find investors. This delayed work till the next year and limited prospecting to Specimen Hill initially with fair results. The Rising Star followed suit and a few years later the group secured further investment with the Ballarat brokers taking shares in the Nuggetty Ajax Company to finally re-open the Nuggetty Ajax mine. TC Thomas was on the board and local mining knowledge was employed.

The local knowledge proved valuable and a few years later the records showed that workings at the mines using foreign practices were showing a loss:

> DAYLESFORD, Thursday - Some figures taken from the report of the Mines department for the December quarter show what has been done by local companies, as contrasted with London managed concerns on the field. The Ajax was floated in 30,000 shares and £9,000 has been called up, no less than £63,750 having been paid in dividends up till 31st December last, thus showing a clear profit of £54,150. The Victorian Cornish has called up capital to the extent of £153,150, has unearthed £102,000 worth of gold and has paid £18,640 in dividends, thus showing an actual loss of nearly a quarter of a million pounds. The Victorian Star has called up £100,000 and has won £10,000 worth of gold. As no dividends have been paid the actual loss is £170,000. The Daylesford Gold Mines Co has called up £120,000 and has won £5,600 worth of gold. As no dividends have been paid, the actual loss has been £125,600. The above figures, taken from the official records, show that over half a million pounds in hard cash has been expended and there is little wonder that the English capitalists fight shy of Victoria. The mines are all right, if the economic Victorian method of working were adopted.

From 1909 to 1917 the North Nuggetty Ajax Company produced 48,000 ounces of gold on its 60 acres at Daylesford. Today the North Nuggetty mine site has heritage significance as parts of the old mine are still in situ.

THE MINERS REST

By the turn of the century, many of the original brokers from The Corner had died. Of those who remained, most were elderly gentlemen with their mining days far behind them. Their families had grown up and spread throughout the country. Many sons and grandsons later went to Europe to serve in World War One. The Exchange in Ballarat was still active and trade in stocks had been extended to new industrial ventures such as the Ballarat Woollen Mills.

In 1907, TC Thomas was resident at the Buck's Head Hotel on the corner of Bridge and Grenville Street in Ballarat, just a block down from the Mining Exchange. The Buck's Head was built by Welshman John Basson Humffray, a lead participant in the Eureka Stockade events of 1854 and one of Victoria's first Parliamentarians. Humffray owned the hotel until 1868 when he fell on hard times after suffering losses on gold mining investments, after which it was sold by creditors. Whilst not quite as popular with the brokers as Craig's Royal Hotel, the Buck's Head was still an imposing building. It found fame a hundred years later after a derailed tram careered into the front of the building leaving a gaping hole and some astonished onlookers. It was demolished in 1960.

Using the Buck's Head as his residential base between mining interests in Egerton, Berringa, and Daylesford, TC Thomas continued to operate his stock broking office at the Mining Exchange, renting space from Joseph Hamilton Dill, an accountant of many years in Ballarat and also the legal manager for TC's Berringa mining companies.

TC's portfolio of shares included the Normanby Gold companies in Ballarat and several syndicate investment companies that bought and leased land to smaller parties in return for gold royalties. Although used by the early squatters for many years, the practice of leasing private land purely for mining royalties was essentially quashed in the early 1900s when the government started cancelling the mining licences of such companies. In theory, this was seen as an opportunity to return the gold leases to working miners rather than mine investors under the umbrella of a royalty making syndicate. In effect, it simply made the mine investors shy and capital for smaller parties harder to obtain. In many respects, the pursuit of gold in Australia by the end of the century had become a web of government regulation, ever changing and almost always in favour of swelling government coffers. However, unlike the mine investors, government just tended to take a clip on the value the gold won without ever getting its hands dirty. Not a public penny was spent on mine development, but the pursuit was taxed at every step.

With Ballarat mining now heavily regulated and prospecting grounds diminishing, the early 1900s saw few new mines open up. The stalwart mines of Seven Hills, Egerton and Berringa were still producing but Ballarat proper offered little hope of new gold. There were a few remaining areas that seemed prospective but not easily tried. One such prospect was the land allocated to the Ballarat Cemetery and in 1907 TC Thomas was heard to have offered £50 to anyone that could secure a mining right within its grounds. Again, and rightly so, the Cemetery was off limits in respect of the dead. Still it was cause for much discussion within the older Ballarat mining community.

In June 1907, TC Thomas fell ill and was constrained to bed in his rooms at the Buck's Head Hotel. Suffering from liver disease, his health deteriorated. On the evening of Saturday 15th of June TC Thomas quietly passed away, a week before his 59th birthday.

From his humble coal mining roots in Wales where he descended the pits at just 12 years-old to his fortunate days at Egerton, Berringa, and Daylesford and very much still an active miner, TC Thomas' 41 years in Victoria had seen him sink a fortune into the Ballarat quartz mines, build a mining empire and circulate in the upper echelons of the goldfields' most respected citizens.

His funeral at the Ballarat Old Cemetery was largely well attended and his pallbearers included his nephew-in-law and chairman of the Ballarat Stock Exchange James Woolcott, Vice Chairman of the Ballarat Stock Exchange William Humphreys, former Mayor and fellow broker

Edward Morey, fellow broker John McDonald MLC, and the then Ballarat Mayor and fellow broker Frederick Brawn MLC.

As a successful gold miner, mine investor, publican, politician, and speculator, as the sun set on a cold winter's day in June 1907 one would expect that TC Thomas' story would end. But it didn't.

GRAVEYARD REEF

GOLD IN GRAVE - DISCOVERY AT BALLARAT

BALLARAT, Monday – While a grave was being dug in the old cemetery, a quartz vein 18in thick and showing gold freely, was cut several feet below the surface. The stone is apparently the cap of a formation. (The Argus, 18 June 1907)

It was business as usual at the Ballarat Cemetery on the cold morning of Sunday 16th of June 1907, when the sexton William Rattray pegged out the gravesite of the latest addition to his list of recently deceased, one TC Thomas: died from exhaustion at the Buck's Head Hotel. In an area no greater than two and a half feet wide by eight feet long he picked up his shovel and started digging. It was possibly the smallest, shallowest hole ever dug for TC Thomas. Soon, a few feet into his dig he struck something hard, a quartz rock formation of some size. It was full of gold.

Respectfully, news of the gold discovery at the Ballarat Cemetery was withheld for a day while an alternative gravesite for TC was found – his final resting place with his mother Amelia just inside the main gates of the Old Cemetery on Creswick Road.

The next day, quartz samples from TC's grave were taken to the School of Mines to be put through the battery. It yielded coarse gold representing an average of nearly two ounces per ton.

On Tuesday the news broke, and the town was suddenly abuzz. The rush to the Cemetery was on. The discovery quickly took the name "Graveyard Run" and became officially known as the Graveyard Reef or Thomas' Run. On Wednesday, James Woollcott announced that the find was "good gold" and several specimens were put on display at the Mining Exchange. By noon that day, five acres of cemetery ground had been pegged out.

The news spread quickly across the country.

DISCOVERY OF A LEADER

Melbourne, June 18 – In sinking a grave in the cemetery at Ballarat North in the neighbourhood of California Hill, a gold-bearing leader was discovered. It is a remarkable coincidence that gold-bearing stone was found in digging the grave of the late Thos. C. Thomas, for twenty years one of the leading mining investors at Ballarat, who had taken a prominent part in developing the golden resources of the Egerton and Berringa districts. (Kalgoorlie Miner, 19 June 1907)

By Friday that week, claims had been lodged on the whole of the cemetery and ground stretching some two miles north. Joseph Kirton MLA, the sitting Member for Ballarat, raced to Melbourne to seek approval to allow prospecting of the ground around the cemetery. By coincidence, his home in Burnbank Street backed onto the cemetery's western edge. Upon his return a few days later, he found that optimistic lease-getters had pegged out all of his property including his house and backyard, to which his voiced his disgust.

Over the coming weeks, the issue of mining rights over "God's acres" was widely debated. The sexton continued to follow the gold vein from TC's original grave 180 feet north, finding it in some places to be five feet wide and only five feet down. More discoveries were made adding no salve to the new gold fever. While many were repulsed by the possibility of important grave sites such as those involved in the Eureka Stockade, and the very thought of any of the 30,000 souls already interred at the Cemetery be in any way disturbed, the lure of gold for some was too great. Night time raids on some of the outer existing burial sites were frequent.

During the rest of June, mining of the cemetery grounds became the main topic of conversation at the Exchange and the wider mining community. Dozens applied for mining leases including Joseph Kirton MLA and TC's friend and Birthday Company manager, Joseph Dill. Dill's area alone encompassed the entire cemetery.

By the end of June, the rulings were in and it was determined that digging within the Cemetery bounds could only be undertaken at no less than 200 feet below the surface, such that none of the burials would be in any way disturbed. This rule is still in effect today.

After the excitement was over, TC's name was eventually added to the headstone of his final resting place, alongside his mother and niece who share the plot. Unfortunately, in the rush to relocate him the cemetery records scribed an error and the stone mason misspelled his middle name, "Thomas Coon Thomas" instead of "Thomas Coomb Thomas" – the middle name he had always loathed.

Perhaps to this day, TC Thomas, William Bailey, Morgan Griffiths, Martin Loughlin, Owen Edwards and the countless other celebrated mining men of Ballarat lay in peace among possibly the largest untouched gold-bearing reefs in the Central Victorian goldfields. Perhaps they smile in the knowledge that they indeed did take it with them - but rest unto God will they lie in their golden grounds forever.

The acquisition of riches is supposed to render men selfish and penurious, but the pioneers of Ballarat have proved an exception to the rule. (Illustrated Australian News, 1 December 1892)

Thomas C. Thomas circa 1880
Gold Museum, Ballarat

Author's note: this portrait is believed to have been painted by Tom Roberts, a noted Australian impressionist painter.

Martin Loughlin
The Australasian, 29 September 1894

William Thomas
The mining managers of Ballarat,
Thomas F Chuck 1826-1898 photographer

William Bailey
The Australasian, April 1 1899

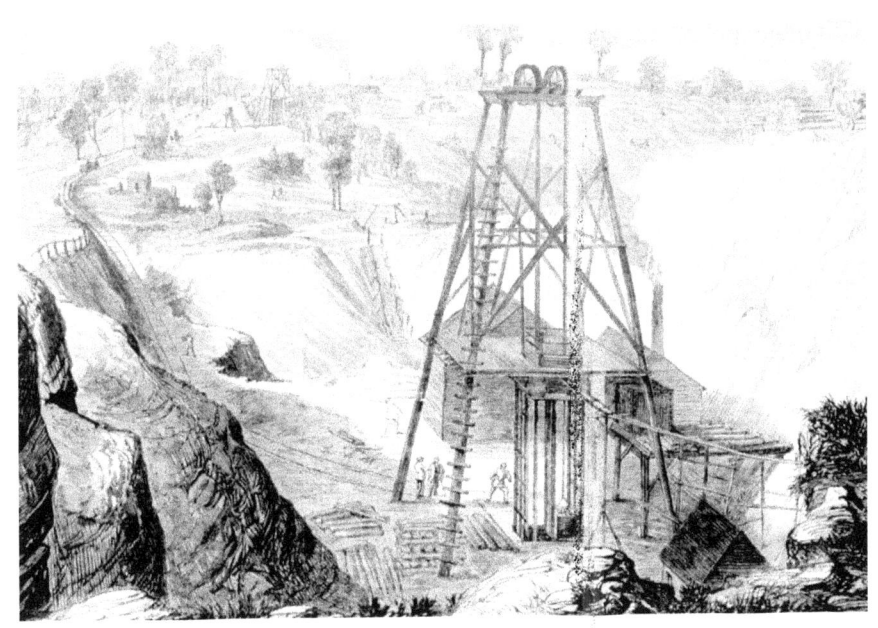

Egerton Mine 1869
Illustrated Australian News for Home Readers, 11 September, 1869

The Nuggetty Ajax Mine, 1923
Geological Survey of Victoria, Bulletins No 42

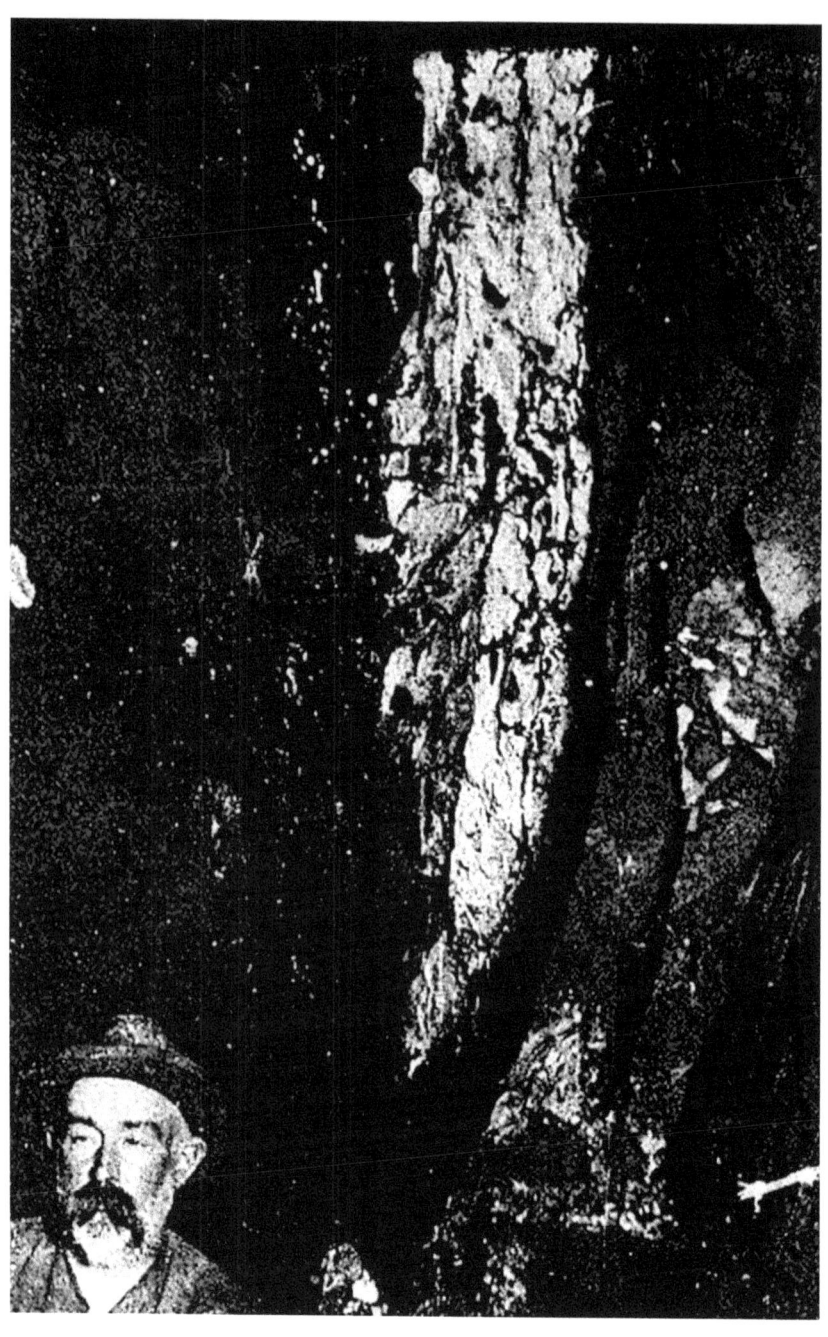

Main Shaft, 1500ft, Egerton Co., 1903
Geological Survey of Victoria, Bulletins No 10

Williams Fancy Mine, Berringa, 1903
Geological Survey Of Victoria, Bulletins No 13

Miners at the face of the reef, 800ft, South Birthday Mine, Berringa, 1903
Geological Survey Of Victoria, Bulletins No 13

The Black Horse shaft at 1760 feet, 1903
Geological Survey of Victoria, Bulletins No 10

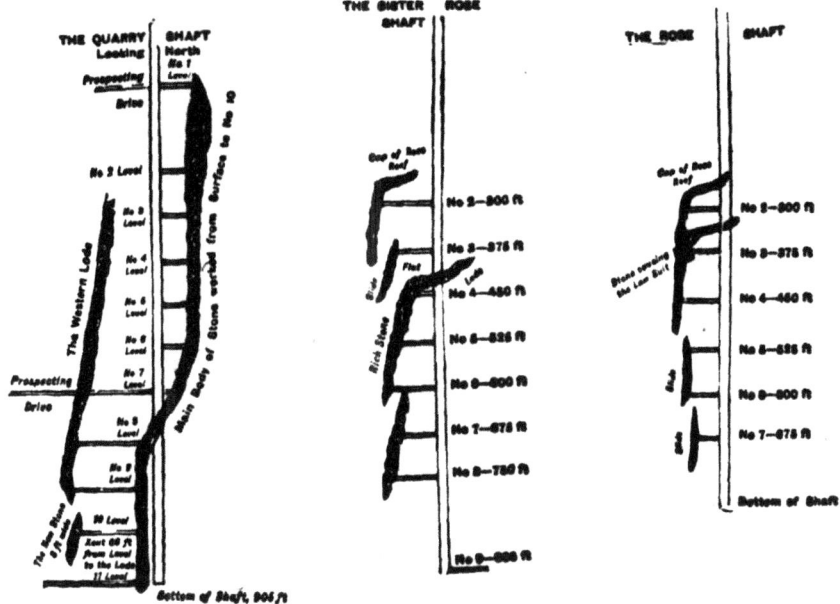

The Egerton Mine shaft diagrams 1885

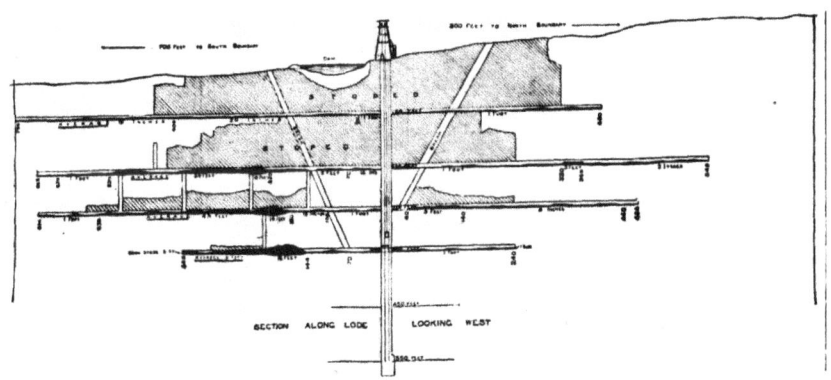

The Birthday Mine shaft diagrams 1900

The Bucks Head Hotel c1890, *State Library of Victoria*

T.C. Thomas gravesite, Ballarat Old Cemetery, *The Australasian*, 29 June 1907

Mount Egerton Mine
Illustrated Australian News, 1 December 1892

The Mining Exchange 1899
Australian Town and Country Journal, 19 August 1899

The Mining Exchange in use as a motor garage c1923
Gold Museum, Ballarat

The Corner, Ballarat 1866
National Library of Australia

The Members of the Ballarat Stock Exchange 1889

Most, if not all, of the founding members of the Ballarat Stock Exchange came from humble beginnings. Many were miners from Britain and Europe, some with experience of the Californian gold rush. As young men in the goldfields of Ballarat's golden heyday, in their blood was an ability to understand and undertake business with the most rudimentary tools. The risks were enormous. There were no computers or spreadsheets, only the necessity to make judgements based on a handshake, act purely on what they saw and heard, draw on their own experience, and make character assessments of untested miners. Trust was key, belief in themselves and those who came to mine paramount. Many fortunes were made – many were lost.

Of the members, many rose to play key roles in the civic and civil establishment of Ballarat and indeed Victoria, often chasing the tail of regulation with innovation. They were charitable men. They prospered families. They built institutions.

The following provides background information on identified members from the official formation of the Ballarat Stock Exchange in 1889.

FREDERICK COURTHOPE DOWNES (1825 – 1902)
Born in Herefordshire, England he came to Victoria in 1853. During his time in Ballarat, he was the legal manager for many mines including the Llanberis Quartz Mining Company. He was also on the board of the Hospital and the Mechanics Institute and was the first chairman of the Bendigo Stock Exchange. His wife predeceased him and he died widowed in Ballarat at age 80.

HENRY (HARRY) RAWLINGS (1828 – 1923)
Rawlings was the son of a printer from Middlesex in England. As a seaman, he arrived in Victoria in 1853, sailing from New York. He was one of the founders of the Mechanics Institute and was a member of the committee for 37 years and treasurer for 27 years. He worked at Eureka prior to the Stockade. A committee member of the Ballarat Stock Exchange, he retired to Melbourne and died in Brunswick at age 95. He never married.

WILLIAM EDWARD WATTS (1838 – 1919)
Born in London, he arrived in Ballarat in 1854 and was a director of the Band and Barton Company. He left for Melbourne in the early 1890s, later advising the Exchange to list lead, silver, copper, and tin stocks, as was done in Melbourne. He was well known for his investments in the Tasmanian copper boom of the 1890s. Affectionately known as "the Doctor", he died in Melbourne at age 81 leaving a wife who passed the following year.

GEORGE HURDIS PURVES (1850 - 1889)
Born in Victoria to English parents, George Purves was a keen investor and sportsman. He was the brother of notable barrister James Purves. At his death he was chairman of the Ballarat Stock Exchange, however, was noted for pursuing his dream to become a novelist. He wrote stories occasionally for The Australasian news journal. He was held in high

regard in literary circles and often wrote for the local papers. He died in Ballarat at age 39 after a long illness, leaving a widow and children.

FELIX MCGOVERN (1830 - 1896)

Born in Ireland, he arrived in Australia in 1850 – one of the first to the goldfields. He ventured to the mines in New Zealand in the 1860s and was chairman of the Black Horse United Company in Egerton as well as holding various other investments. He died, unmarried, in Ballarat at age 66 leaving a valuable estate. Among his benefactors were the Bishop of Ballarat and an amount to enhance St Patrick's Cathedral. Also benefitting were the Ballarat Hospital, Orphan Asylum and Benevolent Asylum, religious orders, various friends and employees and his remaining family in Ireland.

DAVID FITZPATRICK (1829 - 1899)

Born in Ireland, he arrived in the Victorian goldfields in 1851. After working at several diggings, he became a sharebroker in Ballarat in 1866 and was said to have held the position of Honorary Justice in Victoria having been appointed in 1853. He was president of the Lal Lal Turf Club – a position which he held for some 25 years. He died of pneumonia following a bout of influenza at age 70 in Ballarat. He left a widow and several children, one of whom also became a sharebroker.

JAMES DYER WOOLCOTT (1851 – 1918)

Born in Somerset, England, for eight years he followed pastoral pursuits in New Zealand and in Queensland before arriving in Ballarat to work as a miner. He was chairman of the Ballarat Stock Exchange for some 19 years and was also a member of the Melbourne Stock Exchange. A keen interest in public affairs and civic duties saw him become a councillor on the Ballarat City Council, treasurer of the School of Mines, trustee of the Commercial Club, president of the City Free Library, and one of the founders of the Wendouree Recreation Club. He was also a Justice of the Peace and a director of Ballarat Trustees. He married Mary Amelia Valentine (nee Griffiths) daughter of Morgan and Tabitha Griffiths and niece of TC Thomas. He died in Melbourne after a long illness at age 67 leaving his wife and several children.

PETER ERICK PETERSON ALROE (1828 – 1896)

Born in Denmark, as a young man, he served in the Danish Navy where he acquired a medal for bravery. He arrived in Australia around 1857 and married Johanna Casey. Together they had three children in Ballarat. He was naturalised in 1868 and went on to become Mayor of Sebastopol. He died in Ballarat at age 68.

THOMAS BAILEY (1840 - 1914)

Son of a farmer from Somerset, England, he worked for a short time on the New Zealand goldfields before arriving in Ballarat with his family in the late 1850s. A keen angler and yachtsman, he was also involved in horse racing along with his brother William "Weeping" Bailey. He was captain of Ballarat Yacht Club and director of the North Woah Hawp Company. He married Sarah Craig, daughter of Walter Craig, the owner of Craig's Royal Hotel. He died in Ballarat after suffering a bout of asthma.

THOMAS BENNETTS (1828 – 1894)

He arrived in Ballarat before 1862 and he was actively broking at The Corner throughout the 1870s and in Melbourne in the 1890s. He died in Melbourne at age 66 leaving a widow and children.

DAVID BINNIE (1852 – 1902)

A farmer's son and born in Scotland, he arrived in Melbourne in 1854 with his parents at age four. He was in partnership with Thomas Stoddart in the stockbroking firm Stoddart & Binnie and was once secretary of the Ballarat Mining Exchange. He died in Ballarat at age 50 from rheumatic fever. His wife predeceased him.

CHARLES JOHN BARKER (1832 - 1901)

Hailing from Suffolk, England, Charles Barker was the mine manager of the Prince Regent Company, the Northern Star Company and the

Don Company, active miners on the Sebastopol plateau. He was also auditor to the Ballarat City Council and a leading member of the committee of the Anglican Cathedral. His son was also a Ballarat City councillor. He died in Ballarat from heart disease at age 69.

GEORGE BUCKHAM (1832 – 1904)
Born in Newcastle Upon Tyne, England and the son of a sailmaker he took an early apprenticeship in sail making before embarking for Victoria with his parents and siblings in 1852. His father established a tent-making business in Melbourne, however George Buckham ventured west, becoming a stockbroker in Stawell in the 1870s before dealing at Ballarat. He relocated to Melbourne in the 1890s and in 1904, whilst boarding a moving train at Richmond Station, he accidently slipped between the platform and footboard. Being dragged by the train he was subsequently crushed to death. He left a widow and child.

PETER FLETT BORWICK (1841 - 1924)
Born in England, he arrived in Australia in 1867. He was a director of several alluvial mines in the Maryborough district including the Grand Duke and also a shareholder in Ashton's Reef Gold Mining Company. In 1914, he left Ballarat for South Australia where he was a leading member of the Presbyterian Church. He died in Exeter, South Australia at age 83.

FREDERICK WILLIAM BRAWN MLC (1857 - 1936)
Born in Creswick, Victoria to English parents he was educated at the Creswick Grammar School. A broker for some 25 years he was also on the Ballarat City Council and was Mayor for two terms. In 1907 he was elected to the Legislative Council as the member for Wellington Province. He is known for his contributions to the advancement of Ballarat including ensuring a water supply via construction of the Moorabool Reservoir and early afforestation of the area. He was chairman of the Ballarat Water Commission, president of the Ballarat Hospital and vice-chairman of the Ballarat Stock Exchange. He was a

member or the Royal Commission on Closer Settlement and president of the Ballarat High School council.

In sport he was president for many years of the Ballarat Turf Club and District Racing Association; he was a leading spirit in the formation of the Ballarat Golf Club, vice president of the Ballarat Yacht Club and of the Ballarat Choral Union. He died in Ballarat at age 79.

ROBERT STEELE BROWN (1829 – 1908)
Born in Greenock, Scotland and the son of a Presbyterian minister, he came to Ballarat in the early 1850s. He invested in many of the early mines in Ballarat and Bendigo. He died unmarried in Ballarat at age 78.

JAMES BINGHAM (1859 – 1935)
Born at Smythe's Creek, James Bingham ran the broking firm J.G. Bingham & Co in Ballarat before retiring to a farming life in Bacchus Marsh. He died in Bacchus Marsh at the age of 76.

JOSEPH BAIRD (1839 - 1891)
A coal miner from Durham, England, he came to Ballarat in the 1860s and married in 1867. He died in Ballarat at age 52.

THOMAS GREGORY BUNCE (1848 – 1918)
Thomas Bunce was the son of a timber dealer from Devon, England. He arrived in Australia in 1861, settling in Buninyong and was once the president of the Ballarat Stock Exchange. He died in Lismore, Victoria at age 70.

MATTHEW BUTTERLY MLA (1828 – 1893)
Born in Dublin, Ireland, he came to Australia in 1848 via California. He ran a business as a storekeeper and successful hotelier at Waubra. He also established the mill which gave the name to Millbrook near Gordon. He was a considerable investor in the Band of Hope and Albion mines and an early Victorian parliamentarian for the seat of Windermere. He died in Ballarat at age 65 leaving a widow.

ROBERT FORD BRYANT (1841 – 1908)
Son of a copper miner from Cornwall, England he arrived in Ballarat in 1861. Up until his death, he was the mine manager at the Kangaroo Mine in Berringa. He died after a short illness in Ballarat at age 67.

THOMAS BLACKETT (1832 - 1891)
Born in Durham, England, Thomas Blackett made his way to Ballarat in 1854. He married in Buninyong in 1861 and died in Ballarat at age 59.

J BUCHANAN
Details unknown.

RICHARD CLEMENCE (1827 – 1892)
A miner from Cornwall, England he arrived in Ballarat in 1854 with his wife Mary. Apart from his activities as a stockbroker he was also the licensee of the Western Hotel in Sturt Street. He died from cholera in Ballarat at age 64. One of his sons was also a broker at The Corner.

ANDREW CANT (1830 - 1915)
Born in Scotland where his father was the manager of a gasworks. Upon arrival in Melbourne in 1854, he initially worked as a gas fitter and plumber before heading to the goldfields where he married in 1859. He was one of the founders of the Mining Exchange and a shareholder in many mining companies including Ajax Central, Llanberis, Last Chance and New Normanby. He was one of the oldest members of the Mechanics Institute. He died in Ballarat at age 87.

THOMAS WILLIAM COWLEY (1840 – 1914)
Thomas Cowley was from Andreas in the Isle of Man where he worked as a lead miner. He arrived in Ballarat in the 1860s and married. He was also a member of the Ballarat Yacht Club. He retired to Geelong where he died at age 74.

THOMAS COOPER MLA (1832 - 1900)

Born in Staffordshire, England, the son of a draper. He came to Victoria in 1856 where he married. Initially operating a drapery business in Melbourne, he relocated to Creswick where he became active in mining and was a member of Ballarat's Royal Stock Exchange. During his life, he held many influential positions in mining and in politics. He was the first Mayor of Creswick, a position he held for many years. He was elected to the Legislative Assembly in 1877 representing Creswick and was in demand as a speaker and lecturer on mining, education, forestry, and municipal affairs. He died in Creswick at age 68.

GEORGE JOHNSTON CARROLL (1831 – 1890)

Born in Ireland. During his life, he was prominent on many of the shareholder lists and directorates including the New Koh-i-Noor Company, the North Plateau Company, the Northern Star Company, the South Star Company and Owen's & Band of Hope Freehold and Leasehold Company. He was also Chairman of the Star of the East Company and Gay's Freehold Company. In the 1880s, he appears to have formed his own venture in the Carroll Quartz Mining Company and may have invested heavily in the silver deposits of Broken Hill, neither of which bore any success. His co-director of the Star of the East Company and fellow member, Josiah Mager, was a benefactor to his children after his death.

JOSEPH CURTHOYS JP (1832 - 1912)

Born in Bristol, England he arrived in Ballarat the day after the discovery of the first gold. He was the manager of several mines in the district including Llanberis, the Sulieman Pasha Company and the Band of Hope Quartz Mining Company. He had for many years held the position of Justice of the Peace for the Ballarat magisterial district. He died in Ballarat at age 80.

JOHN DITCHBURN (1825 – 1895)

The son of a coal miner and born in Durham, England he arrived in Ballarat in 1850 taking up work as a miner. His parents and siblings followed him to Australia in 1854 and his brother Robert Ditchburn later joined him in his stockbroking business. John Ditchburn later went on to become a member of the Melbourne Stock Exchange. He died in Melbourne at age 70.

MARTIN CHARLES DONNELLY (1837 – 1903)
Martin Donnelly was the son of a farmer from Ireland. In his early life he was educated for the Catholic priesthood, however immigrated to Australia in the 1860s with his father and siblings following the death of his mother in Ireland. His interests in mining extended to mine management as well as having a seat on the Ballarat Exchange. Unmarried, he died in Ballarat at age 66.

WILLIAM ELLIS (1841 - 1918)
Son of a miner and born in Cornwall, England he came to Ballarat in 1858 to work as a miner. He is associated with many of the major mining companies having served as a director on a number, eventually becoming a member of both the Ballarat and Melbourne Exchanges. Known for his charity, he was also a trustee of the Methodist Church. He died in Ballarat at age 75.

EDWIN MILLARD (1838 - 1906)
Born in Somerset, England, he was once chairman of the Ballarat Stock Exchange and was also known for having established its rival the Royal Stock Exchange with fellow broker Thomas Stoddart in 1881. In Melbourne as a member of the Melbourne Stock Exchange, he was known as the "Debenture King" and regarded as "one of the strongest members of the Exchange", an authority of its workings particularly the bond market. He died in Deniliquin, New South Wales at age 68.

OWEN EDWARD EDWARDS JP (1828 - 1905)
Owen Edwards was the son of Captain Owen Edwards, a master mariner from Barmouth in Wales. He arrived in Ballarat in the days of the first gold discoveries in 1852. He held directorships with several Ballarat mining companies including the Prince of Wales & Bonshaw

Company. He is most remembered however for his involvement in the famous Learmonth vs. Bailey case of 1873-1876 surrounding ownership of the Egerton Mine. He was once president of the Ballarat Hospital and the Benevolent Society and was also a founding member of the Old Colonists Association and first Commodore of Ballarat Yacht Club.

A sail maker and carpenter by trade, his obituaries make mention of him being the maker of the Southern Cross flag under which Peter Lalor swore in the men for the Eureka Stockade. He died in Ballarat at age 77, with his investment in the gold mining ventures described as "incalculable".

JOHN EMBLING (1833 – 1895)

A native of Norfolk, England he came to Ballarat in the early 1850s. Along with his life as a stockbroker at The Corner, he was once secretary of the Ballarat Stock Exchange. He was involved as a shareholder, promoter, and director of several Ballarat mining companies and was one of the cooperative parties of men who worked the profitable Prince of Wales and Bonshaw claim at Sebastopol. For many years, he was chairman of the New Koh-i-Noor Company, quartz miners. He was superintendent of St Paul's Sunday school at Ballarat East, secretary of the Orion Lodge of Freemasons and one of the founders of the Holy Trinity Church at Sebastopol. He died in Ballarat at age 62.

E FISHER
Details unknown.

BENJAMIN JOSMAN FINK MLA (1847– 1909)

Born in the Channel Islands he came to Australia in the early 1860s. During his life, he was a prolific investor in the Ballarat mines and in property interests in Melbourne, particularly in the late 1800s. He was also a member of the Legislative Assembly representing Maryborough and Talbot. After suffering an enormous bankruptcy stemming from the Victorian property collapse and loss-making speculations he moved to London where he died at age 62.

ALEXANDER GILPIN JP (1842 - 1905)

A native of Ireland, he arrived in Australia in 1865. As well as being a Justice of the Peace, he was a director of many of the Ballarat and Bendigo mining companies and a member of both exchanges. He died in Melbourne at age 63 and is interred at Ballarat. His son Lt. Alex Gilpin followed him into stock broking and was also a member of the Exchange but died in action during the Boer War.

WILLIAM GRAHAM (1829 – 1906)

Born in Scotland, William Graham was an early investor in the mines of Creswick and Daylesford. Shortly after settling at Daylesford in the 1850s he lost two young children when they wandered off into the bush and were found dead six weeks later. William Graham died in Creswick, Victoria at age 77 leaving a substantial estate including a shareholding in both the Llanberis and The Birthday mines.

WILLIAM GOODALL (1837 - 1911)

The son of a farm labourer from Somerset, England, he came to Australia in the 1860s and was one of the early stockbrokers in Ballarat. His brother, John Goodall (1830 – 1915) was an early broker in Ballarat and later a leading member of the Melbourne Stock Exchange. William Goodall died in Ballarat at age 74.

PHILIP GAY (1829 – 1901)

Hailing from England, Philip Gay arrived in Ballarat in 1853. He was a known investor in many of the Ballarat mines including the Duke of Northumberland Quartz Company which he chaired. He was also a Freemason, a cricketer and was a trustee of the Ballarat Miner's Race Club. He died in Ballarat at age 72.

WILLIAM GALE JP (1836 - 1918)

From the Isle of Man, he was Chairman of the Llanberis Quartz Mining Company as well as being one of the principal shareholders in the Ballarat Banking Co., Ballarat Gas Co., and Ballarat Trustees and Executors Agency. He was prominently associated with a number of

Ballarat charitable institutions including the District Orphan Asylum of which he was a committee member. He was also a judge of Ballarat Yacht Club and in 1890, he became Mayor of Ballarat East. He died widowed in Ballarat at age 71.

J GRIFFITHS
Details unknown.

TENISON GREENE (1840 – 1934)
Irish-born, he arrived in Australia in 1852 at age 12 along with his family. Settling in Ballarat, he became manager of the Emerald Gold Mining Company. He took a position as district surveyor but lost his position in the Black Wednesday public service dismissals of 1878. He spent some 20 years in Western Australia before returning to Melbourne in 1914 where he lived in retirement. He died in Melbourne at age 94 having never married.

HENRY (HARRY) RICHARD GEORGE GODDARD (1855 – 1915)
Harry Goddard was the son of George Goddard, a tailor from Suffolk, England who arrived on the Ballarat diggings in 1851. Harry was a member of the Ballarat Stock Exchange and the Melbourne Stock Exchange. He was a well-known follower of horse racing in Victoria in his later years. His father George Goddard is noted in history as being a participant of the Eureka Stockade in which he was wounded and subsequently arrested in the year that Harry was born. Harry Goddard held the position of director of the Central Plateau Company for some 29 years. He died at his home in South Yarra at age 59.

DAVID HAM (1830 - 1908)
David Ham arrived in Australia in 1849 from Cornwall, England. After working in Geelong, he finally settled in Ballarat where he had some success in alluvial mining. He is noted for having opened the Fryer's Creek gold diggings near Castlemaine. Later Ballarat ventures included running a butcher shop and timber milling. In 1886, he was elected to

the Victorian Legislative Council and was known for his philanthropic endeavours and his prominence within the Methodist Church. He was a shareholder in the Seven Hills Estate Co., vice-president of Ballarat Yacht Club and a committee member of the Benevolent Asylum. He was a known director of the Llanberis Quartz Mining Company, the Last Chance Company, the Northern Star Company and the Leviathan Syndicate Company.

David Ham died at age 77 in Queenscliff, Victoria while on holidays at the home of his son-in-law A.S Baillieu and his remains are interred at Ballarat.

JAMES HOUSTON (1834 – 1899)
An iron miner from Ayrshire, Scotland he arrived in Ballarat with his wife in 1863. Known for his love of bowling and championship expertise in the same, he died in Ballarat at age 65.

JAMES HAMBLY (1844 – 1926)
Born in Cornwall, England he arrived in Australia in 1867 with his wife Rebecca. He died in Camberwell, Melbourne at age 82 and is interred in Ballarat.

WILLIAM THOMAS HUMPHREYS (1858 – 1941)
The son of a blacksmith from Wales, he was born in Ballarat after his parents came to the goldfields in 1854. He was chairman of the Ballarat Gas Company and the Ballarat Banking Company, a member of the board of the Ballarat Trustees Company, and a former chairman of the Ballarat Stock Exchange. For some years, he was on the committee of the Ballarat Orphanage and served as president.

His father Thomas Humphreys was on the board of the Llanberis Quartz Mining Company. William Humphreys died in Ballarat at age 82.

JOHN CLEMENS HICKS (1828 – 1890)
Born in Cornwall, England, his career in Ballarat included directorships of the Llanberis Quartz Mining Company and the New Koh-i-Noor

Company. He was also the mining manager for the acclaimed Band of Hope Quartz Company. He died in Ballarat at age 61.

JAMES HORN (1831 – 1888)
Born in Aberdeen, Scotland he was the son of a farmer. As well as being a member of the Ballarat Stock Exchange he was also a member of the Melbourne Stock Exchange. He died in St Kilda at age 58.

JACOB HUGHES JENKINS (1824 – 1894)
Welsh born; Jacob Jenkins arrived in Ballarat in 1852 to work as a miner. He was a director of Owen's & Band of Hope Freehold and Leasehold Company and landlord of the Garibaldi hotel for many years. He faced the insolvency courts in 1870 (along with Owen Edwards) although by the time of his death he had won back most of his fortune. Reminiscent of his days at The Corner, he was once fined for loitering on the footpath in front of the Melbourne Stock Exchange along with other brokers. He died in Ballarat at age 70. His son Milsom Jenkins was also a member.

MILSOM BOSLEY JENKINS (1860 – 1908)
Born in Ballarat, he became a member of the Ballarat Stock Exchange in his twenties. He later became a member of the Melbourne Stock Exchange during the Broken Hill boom of the 1890s and then following the rise of the goldfields in Kalgoorlie he joined the Adelaide Stock Exchange. He had a keen interest in horse racing and owned a later Melbourne Cup winner. He died suddenly at his home in Glenelg, South Australia at age 48. His father, Jacob Jenkins, was also a member.

SAMUEL PAUL JEFFREE (1841 – 1891)
Born in Cornwall, England, and son of an engine fitter, he came to Ballarat in the 1860s with his parents and some of his siblings and spent many successful years in stockbroking. He died at age 50 in Ballarat.

EDWARD JEFFREY
Details unknown.

HUGH JONES (1826 – 1895)
Born in Wales, he was on the board of the Llanberis Quartz Company and a member of the Old Colonists Association. He died in Ballarat at age 69, just six months prior to his wife Rebecca.

R JONES
Details unknown.

WILLIAM (BILLY) THOMAS JONES (1844 – 1911)
A native of Wales, he came to Ballarat in the early 1860s. Legend has it that his fortune was made when he was given some mining shares on which calls were due on the provision that he made payment of the calls. Not long after, the shares soared in value and William Jones quit digging and went into broking at The Corner. He did well out of the Hurdsfield boom in Ballarat West, and the Madame Berry and Ristori groups of mines in the Allandale district near Creswick. He then went to Melbourne, and on to England where he resided for some time.

Returning to Australia, he became a broker at the Melbourne Stock Exchange before retiring back to England in the 1890s. Among his many investments in Australia were pastoral properties in New South Wales.

He was well known as a racehorse owner. He owned "Bravo", winner of the 1889 Melbourne Cup, and in conjunction with Sir Daniel Cooper raced "Newhaven" winner of the Derby and Melbourne Cup of 1896. He also had success in racing in England. He died in Mayfair, Middlesex, England at age 67.

GEORGE KING (1842 - 1910)
Born in Devon, England, he arrived in Ballarat in 1863 and married in 1867. He is recorded as having been a director of the South Plateau Company and lost a fortune in the 1880s after suffering losses from short selling activities, inadvertently taking several other sharebrokers to the insolvency courts with him. He died after a short illness at his home in Ballarat at age 68.

JOHN LANGDON (1831 – 1913)
The son of a coal miner from Cornwall, England. He was a member of the Ballarat and Melbourne Stock Exchanges, losing most of his wealth in the land and silver boom of the 1890s. He moved to Broken Hill with his wife and children in the late 1880s where he died at age 82.

WILLIAM JAMES LETCHER (1861 – 1947)
Born in Ballarat he became a member of the Exchange along with his father John Letcher and was active in broking throughout the 1890s. He relocated to South Australia in the early 1900s and, with a keen interest in coursing, he became secretary of the National Coursing Club of South Australia. Following retirement to Victoria, he died in Melbourne at age 86.

JAMES LAMB (1836 - 1916)
A native of Glasgow, Scotland he arrived in Ballarat in 1852. He was involved with many of the early mining companies and was also a founding member of the Old Colonists Association. He died in Ballan at age 80.

JOHN LETCHER (1833 - 1916)
The son of a miner from Cornwall, England he came to Australia in the 1850s. He was a foundation member of the Ballarat Stock Exchange and later was also a member of the Melbourne Stock Exchange. He was the manager of the Llanberis Mining Company for many years. He married in Geelong at age 25, was later widowed and then remarried in Ballarat at age 69. He was known as a staunch Methodist and was a local preacher. He died in South Australia at his son's residence at age 83.

MOSES LEWIS (1831 – 1907)
Born in Wales and the son of a coal miner, Moses Lewis came to Victoria with his brothers Lewis and Aaron. He married in Ballarat in 1864 and became a stockbroker at The Corner in the 1870s. He died in Ballarat at age 76.

HENRY LEWIS (1839 – 1904)
Welsh-born, he arrived in Ballarat at a young age. During his life in Ballarat, he was treasurer of the Cambrian Society. He died in Melbourne at age 65 and is interred at Ballarat.

THOMAS LUXTON MLC (1850 - 1911)
Son of a blacksmith, he came to Australia from Cornwall, England in 1852 and settled in Bendigo where he gained knowledge of the mines. He went on the become a founding member of the Bendigo Stock Exchange as well as being a member of the Ballarat and later Melbourne Stock Exchanges. After moving to Melbourne in the late 1800s he entered political life and was a long-time mayor of Prahran, later running several successful businesses. He was also elected to the Legislative Assembly representing South Melbourne and was known for his charitable and philanthropic endeavours. He died in Malvern at age 61.

WILLIAM LITTLE (1839 - 1916)
A native of Cumberland, England he arrived in Victoria in 1851. His early days in Ballarat were spent in the employ of James Oddie before becoming an auctioneer and estate agent on his own account. At the request of ratepayers, he became mayor of Ballarat in 1889 and was the first representative on the Board of Health. He was known for his love of music and art, often showing his collection at the Ballarat Art Gallery. A keen interest in literature saw him write regularly for the local newspapers and his personal work included poetry which he wrote mainly to comfort the bereaved. zHis obituary states that one of his life objectives was to "do what he could to relieve pain and suffering and to offer consolation where needed". He was known for his attention to Ballarat's poor and had a close association with the Methodist Church. He died widowed in Ballarat at age 77.

ALEXANDER LOWENSTEIN (1830 – 1892)
A native of Germany, he was one-time mayor of Maryborough and legal manager for the Duke Group of mines. He committed suicide after suffering financial and legal problems at age 62.

JOHN MCCARTNEY (1836 - 1908)

Born in Ireland he came to the goldfields in the 1860s. He lived most of his life in Ballarat and married in 1878. He died shortly after moving to Melbourne at age 65.

JOHN MCDONALD MCKENZIE (1826 - 1913)

Born in Aberdeen, Scotland, he arrived in Ballarat in 1852. He died widowed at age 87, one of the oldest members of the Ballarat Stock Exchange.

SIR JOHN MCWHAE (1858 – 1927)

Born in Ballarat to Scottish mining parents, John McWhae had an illustrious career. After starting out as a bank clerk, he opened his stockbroking firm in Ballarat then moved to Melbourne in the late 1880s to become a leading member of the Melbourne Stock Exchange including many years as chairman. He was a member of the Legislative Council for 11 years and was an active member in the administration of the Australian Defence Department in the lead-up to World War One. In 1912, he gave his Exchange seat to his son John (who was later killed in France during World War One) to concentrate on his expanding international gold mining ventures as well as his pastoral interests in Queensland, New South Wales, and Victoria. Sir John McWhae was agent-general for Victoria in the early 1920s and was knighted in 1924. He died while on holiday in Japan at age 69.

ALEXANDER MCINTYRE (1830 – 1917)

Born in Londonderry, Ireland he arrived in Australia in the 1850s spending time in Tasmania, New South Wales, and Victoria. He relocated to Melbourne in the 1890s and died in Essendon, Melbourne at age 87.

JOHN YOUNG MCDONALD MLC (1837 - 1917)

Born in Scotland he emigrated lo Australia in 1855. In 1898, he was elected to the Legislative Council representing Wellington Province and held the position until he resigned a few months before his death. He was chairman of the Ballarat Gas Company and a director of the Ballarat Trustees Company, as well as many mining companies, particularly in the Creswick area. He died unmarried in Ballarat at age 80 leaving his large estate to friends and various Ballarat charities. His obituaries note him as "A warm-hearted and manly pioneer, and that he was generous may be concluded when it is learned he left the bulk of his handsome estate to the city in which he made it."

EDWARD MARSHALL MOREY MLC (1832 – 1907)

Born in Kent, England he arrived in Ballarat in 1853 after apprenticing in the merchant navy. He was later a witness to the Eureka Stockade and tended the wounded. His was very successful in gold mining, amassing a huge fortune. He left Ballarat briefly to go the goldfields of New Zealand before returning to become an investor and landowner.

Among his civic activities, he was commodore of Ballarat Yacht Club, a member of the Council of Ballarat Fine Art Public Gallery Association and on the board of the Country Fire Brigade. He was elected to the Legislative Council for the seat of Wellington and in 1894 was also elected mayor of Ballarat. His mining interests included director of the Last Chance Company, Queen's Jubilee Company, Rothschild Company, New Koh-i-Noor Company, Northern Star Company, Egerton No One Company (with Morgan Griffiths and William Bailey) and the Prince of Wales and Bonshaw Company. He was also a member of the Melbourne Stock Exchange. Along with William Bailey and Martin Loughlin he was a member of a syndicate of eight which formed the Seven Hills estate to mine near Creswick. Once considered one of the most wealthy and influential men in Ballarat, he was noted for his inability to read and write. He died in Ballarat at age 75.

WILLIAM MITCHELL (1849 – 1918)

Born in Devon England, he initially went to the goldfields of South Africa and then New Zealand before making his way to Ballarat. In South Africa, he was taken prisoner during the late Kaffir Wars. He died in Ballarat at age 69.

ALEXANDER JAMES EDWARD MOREY (1856 – 1922)

Born in Ballarat, Alexander Morey was the son of Edward Morey MLC. He followed in the footsteps of his father working in mine management. Later he completed an Arts degree at Melbourne University and went on to become a member of the Melbourne Stock Exchange. Known for his love of cricket, he died in Ballarat at age 65.

JOSIAH MAGER (1829 – 1898)

Born in Cornwall, England he arrived in Ballarat in 1852. In his later years, he lived in Geelong amassing a large property portfolio as well as continuing to hold investments in many mining companies. His directorships included the Victoria United Company and the South Star Company, mines on the Sebastopol plateau. He died in Geelong at age 69 and is interred in Ballarat.

T MCGILVRAY

Details unknown.

JOHN MONTGOMERY (1854 – 1935)

Born in London, England and the son of a signwriter, he came to Australia with his family in 1861. He married in 1880. He died in Melbourne at age 80.

WILLIAM NIXON (1834 – 1905)

Born in Dublin, Ireland, William Nixon arrived in Ballarat in the 1850s. He was chairman of the Ballarat Exchange for many years and died in Ballarat at age 71. His wife Anna Maria Cuthbert was the sister of Sir Henry Cuthbert, a prominent Ballarat citizen, and Victoria's solicitor general. As a lawyer, Sir Henry is noted for having led the legal team for the defence in the Learmonth vs. Bailey case over the Egerton Gold Mine.

JOSEPH JEFFCOAT NORTH (1842 – 1906)

Born in Nottinghamshire, England he was a member of both the Ballarat and Melbourne Stock Exchanges. He died in Melbourne at age 63.

E O'REILLY
Details unknown.

JOSEPH POUNDER (1834 – 1917)
Born in Ireland, he arrived in Ballarat in 1862. He died widowed in Ballarat at age 83.

JOSEPH (YOSEF) PHILLIPS (1830 – 1907)
Born in Lambeth, England, he arrived in Australia in 1857. In Ballarat, he formed a produce merchant business under the banner of Phillips and Chamberlain. He was a member of the town council for many years and a founding member of the Old Colonists Association.

At the time of his death, he was treasurer of the Ballarat Benevolent Asylum and on the committees of the Ballarat Orphanage and Ballarat Hospital. He was highly recognised as a charitable man, often providing assistance to the poor and needy from his own pocket. He died in Ballarat at age 77.

WILLIAM MILES PAGE JP (1832 - 1900)
Born in Suffolk, England, the son of a farmer, he came to Australia in the early 1850s. Settling in Melbourne, he married Mary Foreman before heading to the goldfields in the late 1850s. He worked as a legal manager and director for several mines in Ballarat including the Southern Cross Quartz Company. He was appointed as a Justice of the Peace in 1879 and was the mayor of Maryborough in the same period. In Maryborough, he was actively involved in public duties and was associated with the Majorca and Duke mines with colleagues Benjamin Fink, William Bailey and Martin Loughlin. He lost his fortune in the silver boom of the 1890s and later retired back to Melbourne where he died at age 68.

JOSIAH QUILLIAM (1834 - 1897)
Josiah Quilliam was the son of a farmer and native of the Isle of Man. He arrived in Australia in the 1850s. A later member of the Melbourne Stock Exchange, he died in Melbourne at age 63.

RUDOLPH CARL ROEHL (1830 - 1914)

Born in Hamburg, Germany, in his early days on the goldfields he acted as a representative of a German merchant company. He made many mining investments with great success but eventually lost his fortune to bad speculations. He never married. He died accidently in Ballarat at age 84 from injuries sustained after being hit by a runaway horse and carriage in Lydiard Street. He was known as the "father of the Ballarat Stock Exchange".

JOHN SHIELDS REID (1857 – 1938)

The son of a master mariner from England, John Reid was born in Melbourne soon after his parents' arrival in the colony in the early 1850s. Educated at Ballarat College, he later entered the employment of the Union Bank of Australia at Ballarat. His father William Reid and brother James Wilson Reid were also stockbrokers in Ballarat. He joined the Stock Exchange of Melbourne in 1888 and was principal of the firm of Reid and Co share brokers until he retired early in 1927.

In his early years he experienced the market excitement of the Broken Hill silver boom and the Melbourne land boom; at one time he was a director of the Broken Hill Proprietary Company. Later he was interested in Eastern tin-dredging stocks. His obituaries note him as considered one of the most capable operators associated with the Stock Exchange. He died at Mount Macedon at age 81.

JOHN RICHARD RIPPIN (1861 – 1924)

Born in England, after several years at the Ballarat Exchange he later became a member of the Melbourne Stock Exchange, later leaving in the early 1920s to pursue private businesses. He was a well-known philanthropist. He died in Melbourne at age 63.

OLIVER LEWIS RANDELL (1833 – 1899)

A Welshman and son of a shopkeeper, he came to Australia as a miner then working as a sluiceman at the United Albion and Prince of Wales Company, he went on to become a member of the Ballarat, Bendigo, and Melbourne Stock Exchanges. He was one of the early diggers at the

Egerton Goldfield in the late 1850s and was also an early investor in the silver deposits at Broken Hill. He died in Bendigo at age 66.

ANDREW ROBERTSON (1834 – 1920)

Born in the Orkney Islands, Andrew Robertson's career in the mining industry was both extensive and heroic. He attained the position of mining engineer early on and was closely associated with the Victoria United mine in Ballarat and Chalks No 3 mine in Maryborough, although his interests extended to many others as both an engineer and investor.

He is known for his heroism in relation to a major mine disaster at diggings in Rose Hill. In 1869, heavy storms lashed Ballarat causing widespread flooding in the township and corresponding havoc in the deep lead mines. The Great Northern Junction Mine at Rose Hill was inundated with floodwater and 58 men were trapped within the underground drives. At the time, Andrew Robertson was the mining manager and working with the miners in the shafts when he heard the roar of the flood entering the tunnels. He instantly ordered the men to the surface and pushed them into cages as quickly as they arrived. Most got up safely, however, one miner was jammed between the cage and the shaft. Robertson stayed to hoist the injured miner to safety, whilst himself by then being breast deep in water. Including the injured miner, eight miners did not reach the surface and Robertson's concern for their safety saw him forcibly restrained from descending into the flooded shafts to undertake more rescues. For several days, the rescued diggers and the managers, including the directors, frantically tried to pump water out of the mine and during this time Robertson never slept and never once left the spot. After the flood waters dissipated three days later, the men still trapped underground were found alive, save for the injured miner who died moments before rescue and one other who drowned. This flood stands as the second most notable of the mine disasters in Ballarat, the other being the Creswick Mine disaster of 1882 where 22 miners died due to flooding.

After the Great Northern mine disaster, Andrew Robertson continued his mining career taking active managerial positions in a number of

Ballarat mines. He was also a director of the Victorian Life Assurance Company, and later a lecturer in practical mining at the School of Mines. At one time he was actively pursuing an enterprise to develop gold mining in China. He died in Geelong at age 86 and was returned to Ballarat for burial at the New Cemetery.

THOMAS STODDART JP (1829 – 1905)
Born in Roxburgh, Scotland he came to diggings in 1853 and worked as a miner before beginning business as a broker in 1861. Once known as one of the wealthiest men in Ballarat, he travelled extensively throughout Europe bringing back not only 12 Italian marble statues but also the ideas for the establishment of the Mining Exchange, the foundation stone for which he laid and now one of the most iconic buildings in Ballarat. He gifted the marble statues to the City of Ballarat and today they adorn the Ballarat Botanical Gardens. He lost most of his wealth in the banking crisis of the 1890s and died unmarried in Ballarat at age 76. In recognition of his services to the city, a bust of Thomas Stoddart was placed in the City Hall.

SAMUEL WILSON SMYTH (1837 - 1890)
Born in Belfast, Ireland. Along with broking activities in Ballarat, he was also a committee member of the Melbourne Stock Exchange. He died in Melbourne at age 52.

AUGUSTUS SHEPPARD (1822 - 1908)
Hailing from England, he arrived in Australia in 1852. He was the manager of a group that opened the Prince of Wales Mine at Sebastopol and later the Bonshaw mine. A mining injury saw him leave the diggings and join the activity at The Corner. Married twice and widowed twice, he died in Ballarat aged 86.

HENRY SLATER (1834 - 1906)
A farmer's son, born in Cumberland, England, after a career as a sharebroker at The Corner, he retired to Geelong with his second wife. He died in Geelong at age 72.

EDWARD WILLIAM STEPHENS (1829 - 1893)

He was a partner in the firm Stephens and Ruffle, mine managers and a shareholder in many companies including Lone Hand, New North Clunes and Star of the East. In his obituary, he is noted for "having sunk two fortunes" in Ballarat mines. He died in Ballarat at age 64.

JOHN THOMAS SIMMS (1842 - 1908)

Born in Essex, England, after his days at Ballarat he became the mining manager at the Black Range Mining Company in Western Australia. He died whilst mining at Black Range at age 66.

JOHN JAMES SHALLARD (1829 - 1892)

After apprenticing with Bradbury and Evans in London (publishers of Punch magazine), John Shallard came to Australia where he took a position at the Argus and later became one of the founders of The Age newspaper before it became Melbourne's leading newspaper. He then moved to Ballarat to work in the printing department of the Ballarat Star. In Ballarat at age 62, he took his own life after continued losses in mining stocks.

DANIEL SMITH (1816 – 1897)

A native of Worcestershire, England and arriving in Australia in 1855, he was a publican in Ballarat as well as a member of the Stock Exchange. He died in Ballarat at age 82.

STEPHEN TONKIN (1830 – 1906)

He was the son of a miner from Cornwall in England. After his days in Ballarat, he became a member of the Melbourne Stock Exchange and lived with his family in Kew. He returned to Ballarat in the early 1900s where he died at age 76.

FRANCIS (FRANK) THWAITES (1855 - 1900)

Son of an early Creswick pioneer, his father Joshua Thwaites was postmaster at Castlemaine for many years. Frank Thwaites died of typhoid fever at age 45 in Melbourne. His brother Henry (Harry) Thwaites was also a later member of the Exchange.

THOMAS COOMB THOMAS (1848 - 1907)

A coal miner from Wales, he came to Ballarat in 1867 to join his father at the mines in Mount Egerton. From there he followed the gold rush to Gympie in Queensland before returning to take up work at the Egerton Quartz Mine. He is noted for his involvement in the Great Egerton Mine lawsuit of the 1870s. In the 1880s, he ran the Parkers United and Extended companies in Egerton with his partners Henry Morris and Morgan Griffiths. As a mining investor, he provided capital in successful mines such as the Koh-i-nor and Black Horse mines, however, he is most noted for his development of the Birthday mine at Berringa, which went on to become one of the most successful mines in Victoria.

His non-mining pursuits included life as a publican in Egerton and councillor on the Ballan Shire. His sporting interests included horse racing, coursing and shooting and he was a member of the Ballarat Yacht Club. In Egerton, he occasionally sang and played piano recitals to audiences at various private and public functions, and he was active in the civic affairs of the town throughout his life.

He died in Ballarat at age 58 sparking a new gold rush after a gold vein was discovered when digging his grave at the Ballarat Old Cemetery.

JOHN WHYKES (1845 – 1930)

Born in Cornwall, England and the son of a farm labourer, he served as a tailor's apprentice before coming to Ballarat in the 1860s. He is noted as having been twice Mayor of Ballarat. He died in Ballarat at age 84.

HENRY SMITH WYATT (1839 - 1916)

Born in Kent, England he came to Ballarat in 1855 at age 14 with his brother Thomas. While Thomas settled in the Hamilton district, west of Ballarat, Henry initially worked as a miner. In later life, he was associated with the temperance movement. He died in Ballarat at age 78.

MATTHEW WASLEY (1849 - 1908)

The son of a lead miner, Matthew Wasley was born in Cornwall, England before coming to Australia with his family. In the 1880s, he worked the Sulieman Pasha mine where his father Josiah was a manager and they both served as directors on the board of this highly successful company. This mine is noted for having yielded the famous Welcome Nugget.

After the death of his father, Matthew Wasley became a noted investor in the mines in Ballarat, Creswick and Maryborough and was also associated with several public institutions. In his later years he was beset with illness at one point being told that he had just a few months to live; a diagnosis he defied and went on to live for another six years. He died in Ballarat at age 59.

MATTHEW WILLIAMS (1829 – 1913)

A native of Cornwall, England, he was a copper miner at the age of 12. He was one of the early pioneers of the Maryborough district and was a director of the Working Miners Company at Homebush. He lost heavily in the financial crisis of the 1890s and later became a poultry farmer. He died in Sebastopol at age 84.

DAVID WALKER (1841 – 1900)

A native of Glasgow, Scotland, he arrived in Australia in 1856. He was once the manager of the Warrenheip Distillery before becoming a member of the Ballarat Stock Exchange. A consequence of the reduction of the duties on imported spirits, the 1890s saw the award-winning distillery go into gradual demise with many jobs lost. The business was subsequently sold. David Walker died in Ballarat at age 59.

ISAAC WHEELDON (1834 – 1904)

Born in Manchester, England, he came to the Ballarat diggings in 1852. Well known for his lifelong mining association, he was for many years the chairman of the Ballarat Mining Board. He retired to Melbourne in his sixties and died at his home in Elsternwick at age 70.

EDWIN OFFEN WITHERDEN (1832 - 1915)

After apprenticing as a carpenter in Kent, England, he initially went to the Californian goldfields before coming to Australia in 1853. He settled at Mount Egerton and was involved in mining many of the famous deposits around Ballarat including the Black Horse. He went on to become a Justice of the Peace and Ballan Shire councillor and one of the State's early magistrates.

Following retirement, he took up farming pursuits in Gippsland. He died in Melbourne at age 84 and is interred at the Ballarat Cemetery.

JAMES HENRY YATES (1826 - 1893)

The son of a cotton weaver from Lancashire, England he arrived in Ballarat as a miner in 1857. He died in Ballarat at age 68. Twice married, both wives predeceased him.

WILLIAM MURRELL (1835 -1896)

Son of a milliner from England, he was a director of the Band & Barton Company, the North Plateau Company and the Sebastopol Star Company. He died in Ballarat at age 64.

SOURCES

Books, manuscripts, academic papers

Aust. Bureau of Statistics (1947). Official Year Book of the Commonwealth of Australia, No. 11 - 1918, Issue 36

Ballarat Courier. Accessible on microfilm in the Australiana Collection contained in the Ballarat Library

Ballarat District Directory 1869 (L.S. Christie & Co, 1869)

Barnes, E. (2002). Mining directory of mines registered in Victoria: Miscellaneous mining companies' directory 1895-1896 & 1898. Welshman's Reef, Vic: E Barnes.

Baxter, J. G. (1977). Mount of Gold: A brief historical account produced on the occasion of the centenary of the Mt. Egerton Primary School. Mount Egerton, Vic: The School.

Blainey, G. (1969). The rush that never ended: A history of Australian mining. Melbourne: Melbourne University Press.

Bradford, W.M. (1904). Geological Survey of Victoria, No. 13, The Berringa Goldfield (Victoria Department of Mines, 1904)

Cowie, Andrew James (2009). A History of Married Women's Real Property Rights. (Australian Journal of Gender and Law Article, 2009)

Craig's Royal Hotel and its Origins. Craig's Royal Hotel

Evans, T. C. (1887). History of Llangynwyd Parish. Llanelly: Printed at the "Llanelly and County Guardian" Office.

Everist, R. (2006). The traveller's guide to the goldfields: History & natural heritage trails through Central & Western Victoria. Geelong West, Vic: Best Shot! Publications Pty Ltd.

Fitzgerald, F. J. (1966). The Story of William Bailey and the Egerton Mine.

FitzSimons, Peter. (2013). Eureka: the unfinished revolution. North Sydney, NSW. Random House Australia Pty Ltd

Gay, R. (1935). Some Ballaarat Pioneers. Mentone (Vic.: T.H. McBean, Printer)

Griffiths, Peter (1988). Three Times Blest: A History of Buninyong and District (Buninyong and District Historical Society)

J.B. Were & Son. (1954). The House of Were, 1839-1954: The history of J.B. Were & Son, and its founder, Jonathan Binns Were. Melbourne: J.B. Were & Son.

Mansfield, Peter (2002). Ballaarat Yacht Club 1877 – 2002 One Hundred and Twenty Five Years of Yacht Racing on Lake. Wendouree (Ballaarat Yacht Club, 2002)

Menhennet, M. J. (1987). The History of Berringa. Australian Print Group, Maryborough, Victoria

Nixon, Allan M (1991). Stand & deliver! : 100 Australian bushrangers 1789-1901. Lothian, Melbourne

Peter d'Auvergne, Lihir Gold Ballarat (2009), The Deep Lead Mines of Ballarat.

Smith, J. G. (2002). Reminiscences of the Ballarat Goldfield. Ballarat, Vic: Pick Point Pub.

Supple, Ray (1999). Historic Gold Mining Sites In The Southern Mining Divisions Of The Ballarat Mining District

The Cyclopedia of Victoria, Vol.II., (F.W. Niven and Co, 1904)

The Goldfields and Mineral Districts of Victoria R. Brough Smyth (John Ferres, Government Printer, 1869)

Tyler, R. L. (2010). The Welsh in an Australian Gold Town: Ballarat, Victoria, 1850-1900. Cardiff: University of Wales Press.

Withers, W.B (1887). Story of Ballarat (Revised Edition), (F.W. Niven and Co.)

Websites

This book would not be possible without the recent digitisation of Australian newspapers as presented on the National Library of Australia's http://trove.nla.gov.au/. Information on Trove is publicly available, and this book relies on issues digitised up until early 2015.

Australian Dictionary of Biography, http://adb.anu.edu.au

Ballarat General Cemeteries, http://www.ballaratcemeteries.com.au

Births Deaths Marriages Victoria, State Government of Victoria, http://www.bdm.vic.gov.au/

Dictionary of Welsh Biography, http://wbo.llgc.org.uk/en/index.html

Ercildoune Homestead, http://www.ercildoune.com.au/

Eureka Stockade, http://www.australia.gov.au/about-australia/australian-story/eureka-stockade

Gold Museum, Ballarat, http://www.goldmuseum.com.au

Liongold Corp (Berringa mining), http://www.liongoldcorp.com/

Mount Egerton Community website, http://mtegerton.com

Museum of Australian Democracy at Eureka, http://made.org/

Parish of Llangynwyd with Maesteg Plwyf, http://parishofllangynwydwithmaesteg.com

Public Records Office Victoria, http://prov.vic.gov.au/

Segontium Searchers, Genealogy & Local History Research Service (Wales), http://www.segontium.com

St John's Presbytery Dublin Road, Kilkenny, http://www.stjohnskilkenny.com/

State Library Victoria, http://www.slv.vic.gov.au/

The Age Newspaper (digitised history), Google News Archive, https://news.google.com/newspapers?hl=en

Welsh Newspapers Online, http://newspapers.library.wales/

William Abraham (trade unionist), https://en.wikipedia.org

Datasets

Mining Shareholders Index, extracted from the Victoria Government Gazette 1857 – 1886, Marion R.McAdie, (Electronic data CD format, 2006)

http://ancestry.com.au/ - available worldwide data sets as at 2015 including but not limited to: Australia, Death Index 1787-1985, Australia and New Zealand Find A Grave Index 1800s-Current, Australia Cemetery Index 1808-2007, Australia Newspaper Vital Notices, 1851-1997, Australia Birth Index 1788-1922, Australia Marriage Index 1788-1950, Australia Electoral Rolls 1903-1980, Victoria Australia Assisted and Unassisted Passenger Lists 1839–1923, New South Wales Australia Unassisted Immigrant Passenger Lists 1826-1922, Australian Convict Transportation Registers – Other Fleets & Ships 1791-1868, Ancestry.com. Public Member Photos & Scanned Documents, Public Member Stories, Private Member Stories (permissioned access), Australia's Fighting Sons of The Empire. Portraits and Biographies of Australians in the Great War, South Australia Government Gazettes 1867-1884 , Far North Queensland, Australia, Pioneers & Settlers Registers 1825 -1920, Who's Who in Australia, 1921-1950, A Genealogical and Heraldic History of the Colonial Gentry, An Australian Biographical Dictionary, The Dictionary of Australasian Biography, Australian Dictionary of Dates and Men of the Time 1542-1879, The Australian Portrait Gallery and Memoirs of Representative Colonial Men as well as similar datasets for England, Scotland, Ireland and Wales.

Irish in Geelong & District by Pam Jennings & Susie Zada (CD-Rom), September 2011

INDEX

Abraham, Abraham, 53
Abraham, William "Mabon", 124
All Nations gully, 48
Alroe, Peter Erick Peterson, 182
Anderson, Henry, 7
Anglican Cathedral, 183
Bailey Mansion, 107
Bailey, Thomas, 30, 73, 95, 182
Bailey, William, 28, 53, 58, 69, 73, 76, 86, 88, 106, 110, 122, 137, 146, 155
Baird, Joseph, 184
Ballarat Art Gallery, 69, 77, 112, 195, 197
Ballarat Benevolent Association, 129
Ballarat Benevolent Asylum, 77, 110, 191
Ballarat Benevolent Society, 188
Ballarat Cemetery, 161, 163
Ballarat Club, 129
Ballarat Courier newspaper, 44, 54, 112
Ballarat High School, 184
Ballarat Hospital, 77, 110, 188
Ballarat Orphan Asylum, 77
Ballarat Star newspaper, 30, 203
Ballarat Stock Exchange, 67
Ballarat Stock Exchange, Finance and General Agency Company Limited, 69
Ballarat Turf Club, 73, 184
Ballarat Yacht Club, 111, 182, 184, 185, 191, 197
Band of Hope and Albion Company, 56
Band of Hope and Albion Consols Company, 81
Band of Hope Company, 75, 80
Barker, Charles John, 182
Bath, Thomas, 37, 72
Bennetts, Thomas, 182
Bentley's Hotel, 11
Berringa, 155, 185, 204
Big Martin. See Martin Loughlin
Bingham, James, 184
Binnie, David, 69, 182
Birregurra, 46
Birthday Company, 156
Birthday Reef, 157
Black Horse Quartz Company, 85, 102, 127
Black Horse United Company, 181
Black, Charles, 126
Blackett, Thomas, 185
Bluestone arching, 30
Board of Advice, 68
Borwick, Peter Flett, 183
Brawn, Frederick William, 162, 183
Brayton, Edward, 97
Broken Hill Proprietary Company, 141
Broker Licencing Bill, 145
Brown, Robert Steele, 184
Bruun, Ludwig, 116
Bryant, Robert Ford, 157, 185
Buchanan, J, 185
Buck's Head Hotel, 160
Buckham, George, 183
Bunce, Thomas Gregory, 184

Bungal Run, 48
Butterly, Matthew, 184
Cambrian Quartz Company, 30
Cambrian Society, 195
Cant, Andrew, 185
Captain Moonlite, 116
Carroll, George Johnston, 186
Charlie Napier Hotel, 109
Charters Towers, 53, 127
Children's Festival, 57
Chirnside, Andrew, 78
Church of Saint John, Kilkenny, 78
City of Melbourne Bank, 146
Claim jumping, 79
Clarke, Sir John William, 69
Clemence, Richard, 185
Colac Yacht Club, 111
Cooper, Thomas MLA, 186
Corner, The, 24, 29, 36, 61, 65, 70, 73, 85, 87, 121, 127, 130, 160
Cosmopolitan claim, 27
Court of Mines, 64, 79
Cowley, Thomas William, 185
Craig, Sarah, 73, 182
Craig, Walter, 72, 182
Craig's Royal Hotel, 37, 55, 72, 76, 95, 160
Creswick mine disaster, 130
Cumming, John, 107
Curthoys, Joseph, 186
Davis, William, 97
Daylesford mines, 31
Daylesford Mines Proprietary, 158
Dill, Joseph Hamilton, 160, 164
Disher, John, 72
Ditchburn, John, 186
Ditchburn, Robert, 95, 156, 187
Donnelly, Martin Charles, 187
Downes, Frederick Courthope, 69, 180
Duffy Land Acts, 15
Duffy, Charles, 15
Duke Company, 146
Duke, Anne, 112
Dyte, Charles, 115
Eaglehawk mines, 31
Edwards and Davies – Tent and Tarpaulin makers, 109
Edwards, Catherine (nee Hughes), 109
Edwards, Owen Edward, 95, 109, 122, 150, 187, 192
Egerton, 57
Egerton Quartz Mining Company, 50
Egerton Reef, 86
Egerton, George, 48
Ellis, William, 187
Embling, John, 69, 188
Ercildoune, 9, 91, 92, 100
Eureka Flag, 111
Eureka Rebellion, 12
Eureka Stockade, 69, 126
Evans, Robert. See Kangaroo Bob
Evening Mail newspaper, 44
Figgis, C.D., 69
Fink, Benjamin Josman, 146, 188
Fink, Theodore, 149
Fisher, F, 188
Fitzpatrick, David, 69, 181
Foreman, Charles, 100, 127
Fraser, Elizabeth (nee Anderson), 112
Fraser, William AG, 112
Free selection, 15
Frenchman's Lead, 81
Gale, William, 69, 189
Gay, Philip, 189
Geelong Advertiser and Intelligencer newspaper, 113
Gilpin, Alexander, 69, 189
Glengower Estate, 78

Goddard, George, 190
Goddard, Henry Richard George, 190
Gold Fields Commission of Enquiry, 72
Gold production, Victoria, 82
Goodall, John, 189
Goodall, William, 189
Gordon, 21
Graham, William, 189
Graveyard Run, 163
Great Egerton Mine lawsuit, 76, 103
Great Gulf Company, 31
Greene, Tenison, 190
Griffiths, John, 190
Griffiths, Morgan, 29, 53, 58, 86, 95, 110, 118, 136
Gympie, 52
Ham, David, 190
Hambly, James, 191
Hathorn, George, 95
Hayes, Anastasia, 112
Herald and Weekly Times newspaper, 149
Hicks, John Clemens, 191
Highland Clearances, 15
Holy Trinity Church, 188
Horn, James, 69, 192
Houston, James, 191
Humffray, John Basson, 37, 114, 160
Humphreys, Thomas, 191
Humphreys, William Thomas, 161, 191
Investor Protection Society, 68
Jeffree, Samuel Paul, 192
Jeffrey, Edward, 192
Jenkins, Jacob Hughes, 192
Jenkins, Milsom Bosley, 192
Johnson, Anthony, 56
Johnson, Barbara, 56
Johnson, Elizabeth, 56
Johnson, Hannah, 56
Johnson, Joseph, 56
Johnson, Robert, 56
Joint Stock Bank, 146
Jones, Hugh, 193
Jones, R, 193
Jones, William Thomas, 193
Kangaroo Bob, 21, 24, 28, 49
Kangaroo Bob Quartz Company, 23
Kent Villa, 128
Killarney, 78
King, George, 193
King, John, 114
Kirton, Joseph, 164
Koh-i-Noor Company, 81
Lady of the Lake mine, 111
Lal Lal Turf Club, 181
Lalor, Peter, 12, 72, 112, 126, 188
Lamb, James, 194
Langdon, John, 194
Laws of Coverture, 133
Le Page, David, 156
Learmonth brothers, 28, 33, 50, 85, 127
Learmonth family, 13, 16
    Learmonth, Andrew, 90
    Learmonth, John, 90
    Learmonth, Somerville, 7, 90, 92, 95
    Learmonth, Thomas, 7, 86, 88, 90
    Learmonth, Thomas snr, 8, 16, 90
Learmonth Run, 86
Learmonth vs. Bailey, 92, 111
Letcher, John, 194
Letcher, William James, 194
Lewis, Henry, 195
Lewis, Moses, 194
Licenced Brokers Bill, 151
Little, William, 195
Llanberis Quartz Mining Company, 34, 180, 191
Llangynwyd, Wales, 1, 26, 43

Llynfi Valley, 1
Lockhart, Jack, 21
Logs, The, 69
London Chartered Bank, 36, 71
London Stock Exchange, 65
Loughlin, Kathleen, 78
Loughlin, Martin, 75, 92, 95, 106, 122, 150
Loughlin, Thomas, 78
Lowenstein, Alexander, 146, 195
Luxton, Thomas, 195
Mabon's Monday, 124
Mager, Josiah, 198
Majorca Lead, 146
Married Women's Property Act, 135, 149
Matthews, Peter, 110
McCartney, John, 196
McDonald, John Young, 70, 162, 196
McGilvray, T, 198
McGovern, Felix, 69, 181
McIntyre, Alexander, 196
McKenzie, John McDonald, 196
McWhae, Sir John, 196
Mechanics Institute, 110
Melbourne Club, 13
Mercantile Finance and Guarantee Company, 147
Methodist Church, 187, 191, 195
Midas Tribute Company, 31
Millard, Edwin, 66, 187
Miners' Federation of Great Britain, 124
Mining Companies Limited Liability Act, 25, 62
Mining Exchange, 37, 69, 144, 155
Mitchell, William, 197
Monmouthshire and South Wales Conciliation Board, 124
Montgomery, J, 198

Morey, Alexander James Edward, 198
Morey, Edward Marshall, 69, 95, 110, 146, 162, 197
Morning Light, 43
Morris, Henry, 95, 100
Mount Britten (Queensland) Gold Mine Limited, 65
Mount Buningyong, 7
Mount Egerton, 17, 21, 28, 34, 46, 48, 121
Mount Egerton Hotel, 22
Mount Egerton Steam Puddling Company, 88, 100
Munro, James, 147
Murphy, Barney, 22
Murray, John, 69
Murrell, William, 206
Nazareth House, 76
New Australasian mine, 130
New Enterprise mine, 28, 33, 45
Nimblefoot, 74
Nixon, William, 198
Normanby Gold, 160
North German Quartz Company, 31
North, Joseph Jeffcoat, 198
Nuggetty Ajax, 158
O'Reilly, E, 199
Oddie, James, 195
Old Colonists Association, 69, 110, 129, 188, 194
Page, William Miles, 199
Park Hall, Stirlingshire, 16, 90
Phillips, Joseph, 199
Potato Famine, 15
Pounder, Joseph, 199
Presbyterian Church, 183
Prince Alfred, 55
Prince of Wales & Bonshaw Company, 188
Prince of Wales Company, 81

Prince of Wales Hotel, St Kilda, 73
Punch magazine, 203
Purves, George Hurdis, 69, 180
Quarry shaft, 85, 102
Queen Victoria Quartz mine, 30
Quilliam, Josiah, 199
Randell, Oliver Lewis, 100, 126, 200
Rattray, William, 163
Rawlings, Henry, 70, 180
Red Hill Lead, 80
Red Streak claim, 33
Reform Company, Haddon, 31
Reform League, 37, 72, 113
Reid, James Wilson, 200
Reid, John Shields, 69, 200
Reid, William, 200
Rippin, John Richard, 200
Robertson, Andrew, 201
Roehl, Rudolph Carl, 200
Rose shaft, 85, 102
Royal Stock Exchange, 67, 187
Royal Stock Exchange Hotel, 122
Russell, Alexander, 48
Salting scandal, 68
School of Mines, 163, 181
Scobie, James, 11
Seekamp, Henry, 113
Seven Hills Estate, 76, 106, 191, 197
Shallard, John, 203
Sheet Anchor, 77
Sheppard, Augustus, 202
Shiels, William, 147
Silver boom, 141
Silver standard, 142
Simms, John Thomas, 203
Sister Rose shaft, 103
Slater, Henry, 202
Smith, Daniel, 203
Smoker, 21
Smyth, Samuel Wilson, 202

South Birthday mine, 108
South Wales Miners' Federation, 124
Southern Cross flag, 112
Specimen Hill, 158
Spread Eagle claim, 33
Squatters, 9, 13
St John of God's Hospital, 108
St Patrick's Cathedral, 76, 181
St. Cynwyd's Church, 1
St. George and Band of Hope United Company, 81
Staffordshire Reef, 106, 155
Stamp duty, 145
Star newspaper, 44
Stephens, Edward William, 203
Sticky Hop, 127
Stoddart, Thomas, 36, 69, 156, 182, 202
Syme, David, 28, 49, 126, 149
Tanner, Ralph Wing, 100, 106, 123
Tattersall's Hotel, 72
Terrinallum Station, 107
The Age newspaper, 49, 126, 149
The Australasian newspaper, 180
Thomas family
    Thomas, Amelia, 2, 27
    Thomas, Mary, 58
    Thomas, Tabitha, 2, 43, 58, 136, 156
    Thomas, Thomas Coomb, 2, 27, 43, 51, 57, 94, 95, 108, 122, 127, 150, 155, 158, 163, 204
    Thomas, William, 2, 27, 28, 43, 53, 86
    Thomas, William Powell, 2, 45
Thomas, Bill. See Thomas, William Powell
Thomas' Run, 163
Thompson, Mary, 111
Thwaites, Francis (Frank), 203
Thwaites, Henry, 204
Tonkin, Stephen, 203

Unicorn Hotel, 24, 36, 71
Vern, Frederick, 126
Victorian land banks, 145
Victorian Mining Accident Relief Fund, 130
Voluntary Liquidation Act, 142
Walker, David, 205
Warren, George, 94
Warrenheip Distillery, 205
Wasley, Matthew, 205
Watts, William Edward, 70, 180
Waverley Park, 8
Weeping William Bailey. See Bailey, William
Welsh Eisteddfod, 110
Wheeldon, Isaac, 205
Whykes, John, 204
Williams, Matthew, 146, 205
Williamson, James, 92, 97, 137
Winter, Jock, 8
Winter-Irving, William, 78
Witherden, Edwin, 85, 100, 122, 126, 146, 150, 206
Withers, Anne, 112
Withers, William B, 45, 112
Women in the goldfields, 132
Woolcott, James Dyer, 161, 181
Wyatt, Henry Smith, 126, 204
Wynne, Agar, 107
Yates, James Henry, 206
Yelland, Isaac, 21
Yuille Swamp, 8
Yuille, Henry, 7

www.ingramcontent.com/pod-product-compliance
Ingram Content Group UK Ltd.
Pitfield, Milton Keynes, MK11 3LW, UK
UKHW021313180426
11947UKWH00015B/1199